The Crusades

www.pocketessentials.com

Also by this Author
Ancient Greece

The Crusades

MIKE PAINE

POCKET ESSENTIALS

This edition published in 2005
by Pocket Essentials, a division of Oldcastle Books
P.O.Box 394, Harpenden, Herts, AL5 1XJ
Reprinted 2011

www.pocketessentials.com

© Mike Paine 2005

The right of Mike Paine to be identified as the author of this work has been asserted
in accordance with Copyright, Designs and Patents Act 1988.

A CIP catalogue record for this book is available from the British Library.

ISBN 13: 978 1 84243 564 9

2 4 6 8 10 9 7 5 3

Typeset by Avocet Typeset, Chilton, Aylesbury, Bucks
Printed and bound in Great Britain by Cox & Wyman, Reading, Berks.

Acknowledgements

This book would have been impossible without the entirely superior work of Sir Steven Runciman, to whose magisterial history this slight thing is vastly indebted.

On a personal and professional level, thanks are due to the immeasurable support given by my family (particularly Joshua and Caspar); Francis Cleverdon; John Shire; my editor, Nick Rennison; and fellow-traveller and greyhound-enthusiast, Sean Martin. Belated thanks also go to John Parish for his help in a previous work to the Crusades, one no less bloody and ultimately as unsuccessful, but one that would have been far less enjoyable without his contribution.

For the second edition, I would like to – in addition – thank the following: Parveen Adams, Paul Baggaley, Ian Brereton, Suparna Choudhury, Mark Cousins, Paul Gibson, Dale Grundle, Terumi Kawasaki, Vicky Lebeau, David Marriott, Martine Roberts, and Andrea Ughetto.

All errors are, needless to say, entirely my own – *Deus lo volt*.

Contents

Prologue: The Last Crusade

WASHINGTON (Reuters) – Years after President Bush set off alarm bells in the Muslim world by referring to his war against terrorism as a 'crusade', the word that Arabs equate with Christian brutality has resurfaced in a Bush campaign fund-raising letter, officials acknowledged on Sunday...

The March 3 letter, which Bush-Cheney Campaign Chairman Marc Racicot sent to new campaign charter members in Florida, lauded the Republican president for 'leading a global crusade against terrorism' while citing evidence of Bush's 'strong, steady leadership during difficult times'.

However, the word 'crusade' recalls a historical trauma for the Muslim world, which was besieged by Christian crusaders from Europe during the Middle Ages.

In the weeks following the September 11, 2001, attacks on New York and Washington, Bush caused an uproar by telling reporters: 'This crusade, this war on terrorism, is going to take awhile.' Faced with worldwide consternation over the remark, the White House later said Bush regretted his use of the term.

On Sunday, Racicot said… 'That letter was focused upon the single-minded efforts of the president, in coalition with other members of the international community, to undertake a mission to liberate people and protect the cause of freedom — not just for a moment, not for a day, not for 10 years but for 100 years,' the former Montana governor said in a conference call with reporters…

Some words, some images, like wars, won't be easily forgotten. The football terrace chant of *Two World Wars and One World Cup*, Basil Fawlty goose-stepping in an episode of *Fawlty Towers*, Spielberg's *Saving Private Ryan* – the conflicts of the past refuse to slip away quietly. Turning on the radio the listener finds a discussion between academics on the question of holding present-day Germany responsible for the crimes of previous wars. In the build-up to an England-Germany football match a tabloid newspaper paints the event in military colours. Sometimes in the public arena, when the subject of Germany comes up, nagging voices urge us to remember the past. Whatever today's Germans are like, they seem to be saying, we must always remember the crimes of their forefathers. Germany is somehow stained indelibly by these crimes. Unremarkable acts on Germany's part in the European Union are likely to be viewed by these same commentators as likewise stained by these crimes. It is assumed that unspeakable motivations lie beneath the surface. Any act of German self-interest might be a resurgence of old desires for control of Europe.

Britain, too, is not immune to these kind of accusations: some people responded to recent criticisms of the current regime in Zimbabwe as if a concern for human rights was merely a cover for old imperialist urges. Perhaps a few old men in both Germany and Britain quietly long for an imperial past – but certainly each year that passes buries more and more of these dreams.

Curiously, the nightmares of old enemies outlast the memories of old allies. France may have faced Germany in the Second World War; there might be much talk of the entente cordiale. Yet a similar although milder distrust hangs over the French. *Remember Napoleon!*

But what has this to do with the Crusades? After so many centuries, who can really care about them besides historians, or those who enjoy a good military tale? Britain, after all, has put both the Roman and Viking invasions behind it. We appear to have forgiven Scandinavia and Italy a long time ago. What is it then about the word *crusade* that can cause such anxiety? Isn't it just, as the dictionary describes it, 'an energetic and organised campaign motivated by a fervent desire for change'.

Perhaps this was George Bush's (or at least his advisors') understanding of the word when he famously called for one against terrorism. Yet we must reflect that the choice of the word was particularly apposite on this occasion, despite Bush's attempts to retract it. After all, both George Bush and Tony Blair are characterised by their Christian faith, and their opponents in this case are followers of Islam. And haven't we witnessed an invasion of parts of the Middle East by a force that is comprised of countries that are either European (Spain and Britain for example) or inheritors of a European cultural and political tradition (the United States and Australia)? And weren't both enterprises supported by the best of motivations in their times and contexts: freedom on the one hand, Christianity on the other? And *surely* someone in the White House must have been aware of the parallels between the leader of the most powerful country in the world calling for a crusade in 2001, and the head of the Christian church calling for a crusade nearly a thousand years before?

So one can understand why the word was used. Indeed if any activity has the right to be called a crusade in the modern age, perhaps this one is it. The problem was less the White House's understanding of the word and more their understanding of what it meant for others.

The historical Crusades mark an interesting and important period in the development of Europe. It is an early stage in the development of the European nation-state, and an early stage of the development of the involvement of Europe in the affairs of the rest of the world. In later centuries many of the states of Europe became heads of rich and powerful empires, and this wealth and power was due in a large part to their exploitation of much of the rest of the world. So we can perhaps see the Crusades as the first, tentative steps towards empire. Crusaders saw themselves as doing God's work. In a similar fashion those who followed much later saw themselves bringing civilisation to the savages. Economic benefits accompanied both. Despite the cost in men and goods some historians have argued that the wealth coming into the Italian city-states during the Crusades, through both easier trade and through conquest, helped kick-start the Italian Renaissance.

So despite the enormous passage of time, a distance that might dull the memory of the human cost to the Middle East of the Crusades, or that might reduce the anger at the memory of the invasions, the image of the Crusades as the start of a long process of exploitation, of rule by the West of the rest of the world, brings them closer to the modern era.

In another way, too, some conquests, some wars, are more easily forgiven than others. The invasions of England by the Romans, by the Vikings, by the

Normans, all ended with assimilation. Indeed the great success of the Roman Empire can be attributed to the manner in which the Romans consciously sought to merge their own culture with the cultures of those they had conquered. But the Crusades were based, just as later imperialist conquests were, on ideas of segregation. The Crusaders, of different races and languages, were unified by one thing – their Christian faith. And there was no possibility of a compromise here. One was either a Christian or one was not. This was a defining moment in the historical development of the relationship between Europe and the rest of the world. On one side are the Europeans, who are Christians, and, on the other, the natives who are inferior because of the very thing that most identifies them – their religious belief.

A third development has helped the word retain its potency. The establishment of the state of Israel in 1948, whilst bearing no relationship to the acts and intents of the Crusaders, is still, in the eyes of some, the symbol of a loss which resonates with the crusading period. Israel was formed subsequent to the brief British rule of Palestine (it came under British control after the First World War following centuries of rule by the Ottoman Empire) and the main foreign source of financial support for Israel in the present day is the United States. To some Muslims these facts again echo and recall the involvement of the West in the Crusades. Such determined misreadings, as we earlier saw, are not exclusive to the Middle East.

So the word *crusade* remains extraordinarily potent – in some parts of the world at least. Indeed it is in the nature of history itself to support such associations between periods. Every war has its reasons, and its legacies; and one can never disentangle the past from the present with ease. Any book that brings an historical period to life does so in part by linking it to the present. Long-dead figures come alive to us when we see their similarities to us; their motivations are ones we understand. Our understanding of the terror of the Assassins felt by the inhabitants of the Crusader states – the fear that at any moment, in a public place, careless of their own survival, a terrorist might strike – is grimly brought to life by today's terrorist attacks. On the other hand we sometimes struggle to see the similarities between the period we are living in and the past. In a few hundred years historians will look back and judge whether we are living today in crusading times. Let us at least hope that if we are, they are brought to a conclusion with greater alacrity than was the case with the original enterprise. Marc Racicot's state of freedom that lasts for a hundred years has less comforting associations than he realises. And what will happen then?

But let us now go to the source of all this confusion.

PART 1

The Islamic World and the East

The Islamic World and the East

Centuries of dust covered the fabulous gardens of Haroun al-Rashid, Caliph of Baghdad, Commander of the Faithful. The splendour of the barges that conveyed him down the Tigris at night with his faithful wazir, Jafar; the anonymous walks with his sword-bearer, Masrur, among his subjects in the morning market place – these tales were told by storytellers on the streets of medieval Damascus and Cairo, and in the souks of Baghdad itself. Haroun, like his Frankish contemporary Charlemagne, was a figure who slipped out from between the covers of history and passed into myth. In these stories, eventually to make their way into the *Alf Layla wa-Layla* (frequently translated into English as the *Arabian Nights*, although a more literal translation would be *The Thousand Nights and One Night*), the political security of al-Rashid's reign appears in the opulent settings of palaces and merchant caravans and endless, lush detail. Whatever the realities of life at the end of the 8th century under Abbasid rule, it was, in retrospect, a golden age. To an audience in the schismatic and politically-divided

Middle East of the 11th century it would not have been difficult to accept the wealth of these tales as the fruit of a Muslim world unified under one leader sanctioned by God: the Dar al-Islam.

For the divided state of Islam is at the heart of the early successes of the Crusades. The first three centuries after its irruption among the Arabs and Bedouin of the Arabian peninsula had seen Islam spread rapidly across a major part of the ancient world. Most of Arabia had converted by the time of the death of Mohammed in 632 AD. Those old Empires, Byzantine and Sassanian, which had spent so long quarrelling over their shared Near East hinterlands, were in turn driven back by these converts. Jerusalem was to surrender in 638. By 640 the Romans had lost Syria. Egypt had fallen by 646. By 651 the last Sassanian Emperor – Yazdegerd III – and the four-hundred-year-old empire he had ruled had passed into history. So territories fell in turn, as North Africa – the Maghrib – was overrun up to the very gateway to Western Europe. By the middle of the 8th century, even Iberia (modern Spain and Portugal) was occupied by an army comprised of Arabs and the Muslim converts of the Maghrib, the Berbers. There were occasional raiding parties that came over the Pyrenees. The significance of the defeat of one such party by Charles Martel (Charles the Hammer) in 732 grew with the telling until it became known as the epic battle that saved Europe from a final and complete conquest by the Infidel. But apart from these raids, this was the Islamic world, the Dar al-Islam, unrolled across the map as far as it would go.

The conquest of the Maghrib had involved the annexation of Byzantine cities such as Carthage. Beginning with the conquest of Syria, Muslim forces worried away at the eastern half of the Byzantine Empire for the next eighty years, inevitably ending up by laying siege to the capital, Byzantium, in 674 and again in 717. The earlier siege was finally repelled after four years, partly due to the Byzantines' unique weapon, Greek fire (a liquid whose recipe has been lost but can perhaps best be described as medieval napalm). The Byzantine Empire, which had thrived and spread across the coastal areas of the Mediterranean as a consequence of its uncontested command of that sea, now found itself increasingly challenged by both Islamic navies and Islamic pirates. It was, in part, the contest between these two great cultures that was to lead eventually to the First Crusade.

Who were the Byzantines? The name itself is slightly deceptive. Their origin was Roman, and their story is in part the answer to the question of what happened to the Roman Empire. The origin of Byzantium itself was as a Greek colony founded in the 8th century BC. For hundreds of years it remained a provincial centre, only rising to prominence when the first Christian Roman Emperor, Constantine I, on ascending to power in 324 AD, chose to make it his capital instead of Rome. This *New Rome* soon took on its founder's name, and thus was Constantinople born. As an imperial capital, the fortified city rapidly grew both in size and strength. Time passed, and the Empire divided: tucked away at the edge of Europe, the Roman Empire of the East was to avoid the barbarian hordes that finally overwhelmed Rome.

As the Empire of the West receded into memory, the East gradually found its own path of development. By the medieval period its blend of Eastern cultural sophistication, the particular route its Christianity had taken both in ceremony and belief, and its Roman inheritance had justified a new description by historians as Byzantine. This Empire was to become a beacon shining at the edge of Dark Age Europe, a very real link with the Roman world that would last until Constantinople was finally conquered by the Ottoman Turks in 1453. The Byzantines may have seen themselves as the continuation of Rome, and perhaps as the safeguard and continuation of all that was truly civilised in Rome. They were maintaining Europe's great old civilisation. But this cultural gap (one that only grew with the passing centuries) and their physical position at the edge of the continent only rendered them increasingly foreign, non-European in the eyes of the European kingdoms that were to form out of the barbarian invasions. Ironically, it was only towards the end of their empire, with the rebirth of interest in the classical world in Italy that is known as the Renaissance, that in a sense the lonely light that Byzantium had kept burning over the long centuries finally spread back to the old territories of Rome.

The Empire radiated out from the hub of Constantinople. At its core was always Asia Minor and Thracian Greece, below the Danube. Added to these lands were much of the North African coast, Egypt, Dalmatia (modern Yugoslavia), Southern Italy and Sicily. At its eastern marches were the Sassanids; to the west, the tribes of the Balkans. A constant feature there was the pressure from nomadic peoples moving from Asia into Europe, and driving forward those they found before them. In the east the replacement of the Sassanids by the Arabs only served to increase Byzantine difficulties.

The siege of 717 AD however, represented the pinnacle of Islamic ambition where Constantinople was concerned. The Arabs were repelled and while they continued to make incursions into Byzantine territory time saw increased fragmentation within their ranks. The Umayyad Dynasty had held total control of the Islamic World from 661 to 750. The subsequent rise of the Abbasids still left them the Emirate of Cordoba – most of modern Spain and Portugal – after losing the rest. With the Abbasid ascension the capital passed from Damascus to Baghdad. By the tenth century the Abbasids, too, were in decline with many autonomous Muslim states appearing across the Maghrib and the

Near East. The Byzantines made the most of this political disarray. The Abbasids held power to the east; a rival dynasty, the Fatamids, held the Maghrib. From 945 the Byzantines marched out under a variety of rulers and took back many of the cities of the Levant that were under the control of the minor Muslim rulers, and successively confronted the Fatamids and Abbasids.

By the 11th century, to all intents and purposes, a general truce held between the three major forces. As was often to prove the case later on, the enmity was greater between the two Islamic sides than between either of them and the Byzantines. Jerusalem remained under Islamic control and had done ever since its surrender to the Caliph Omar in 638 AD. The Christians there, as was commonly the case elsewhere, enjoyed reasonable treatment under the Muslims. The latter were prepared to allow Christian and Jewish practice to go on as recognition of the status of these two religions as *ahl al-kitab*, People of the Book. Indeed all three religions were connected. As Christianity had its roots in Judaism, so Muslims accorded Jesus the position of prophet — all could be seen as worshipping the same god in essence. This relationship meant that Christians often and easily converted to Islam — it was not difficult to argue that the latter was a more advanced form of the former. The tolerance shown to these faiths by the Muslims was not without a cost — literally so. A tax, *jizyah*, was payable by all who were allowed to follow these divergent beliefs. It was this payment, and the obvious advantages of following a religion that was indivisible from the political power in these countries, that were further strong incentives to convert when spiritual arguments proved insufficient. The enormous expansion in the numbers of believers that followed such conversions brought a cultural and social variety that both strengthened and weakened the Islamic world. In the short term an immediate problem were the taxes lost when so many did convert. In the long term the greater diversity in backgrounds between Muslims proved more problematic. Factionalism had been a problem when the religion had been an entirely Arabic affair. How much greater was the scope for division when so many different cultures now described themselves as Islamic. Islam's great strength in its early period of conquest had been its unity – shared beliefs, a shared culture. Now different communities within it had their own interests to promote and protect.

These inner tensions were not unique to Islam: the Byzantine Empire was frequently riven by its own brands of dissent. The most notorious was the enormous controversy that raged over whether or not religious iconography was acceptable. For most of the 8th century strife occurred between those who used icons and those who were fervently against them. Beside these social conflicts were more personal disputes: the family conflicts and treacheries that had so often bedevilled the Caesars were not unknown to their Byzantine descendants. But not everything was about differences. The blend of Greek, Roman, Sassanid and Persian civilisations existing in the East made for a sophisticated culture that was common to both Byzantine and Muslim. Not only did the Byzantines preserve Roman and Greek civilisation. The scholars of Islam also prevented the loss of much Ancient Greek thought and, in addition, had their own contributions to make – in the field of mathematics, for instance. Much divided the two civilisations but much united them too. In comparison, the societies of Western Europe at this time were indeed those of barbarians, living in colder climates at the edge of the world.

So the condition of Christians in the Holy Land in the 11th century was by no means intolerable. True, Jerusalem was still held by the Fatamids. In practice, however, the toleration shown to many of the differing Christian cults in the East was greater than they would have received from their supposed brethren. Both the Byzantine Orthodox Church and the Roman Catholic Church attempted at times to wipe out divergent practices and beliefs; Muslim rule protected these Eastern Christians from such attempts. Yet against the occasional desire of the Orthodox Church to control their practices, a strong and Christian empire at the border of the Islamic world must have also reassured the Christians living under Muslim rule to some extent. While the Muslims tolerated them life was not that bad and, if things took a turn for the worse, they didn't have far to go to seek sanctuary. This balance and understanding between the two civilisations, far from secure though it was, allowed for a peace that benefited more than just the people of both empires. Daily life was safe enough for pilgrims from distant Europe to journey to Jerusalem and the other holy sites in relative security. Yet something was to upset the balance.

The Seljuk Turks were recent converts to Islam, coming out of Turkestan in central Asia. Turks had featured as Abbasid mercenaries for a while, with a fearsome reputation. Under their leader, Tughril Beg, they had supplanted Abbasid rule. After his death in 1063 his successor, Alp Arslan, embarked on a series of campaigns against the Byzantines. After a number of other victories, the Turks conquered Armenia, an independent, Christian state that had recently gone over to the Byzantines. The stage was set for a decisive confrontation between Christian and Turk.

It came in 1071. The Battle of Manzikert was one of the blackest days for the Byzantine Empire. A large Byzantine army that included many mercenaries – Normans, Vikings, Slavs and indeed Turks (an unwise addition to the forces since they defected at a crucial moment towards the end of the conflict) – was comprehensively crushed. The Emperor, Romanus Diogenes, was captured. While the Turkish command did not seek immediately to press the advantage, the opportunity was later taken up by others – nomadic Turks seeking land on which to settle. These, led by Suleiman ibn Kutulmish, started making inroads into Byzantine territory in Asia Minor from 1073. Jerusalem was taken from the Fatamids in the same year that the Battle of Manzikert took place. Turkish adventurers sprang up everywhere, taking land from either side. Chaos ensued. The steady stream of pilgrims from Europe now dried up – the traveller who dared to make his way over the traditional land routes was frequently prey to a group of marauding bandits.

After Manzikert, much blame remained for allocation and Constantinople saw feuding among its ruling classes until the emergence of Alexius Comnenus, who saw clearly that his most pressing task was to bring the Empire back from the brink. With the Turks to the east, the Bulgars to the west, and the recent loss of southern Italy to the Normans, the Empire was in a perilous position. As he played off minor Turkish chiefs against each other in a struggle to ensure the Empire's survival, Alexius was all too aware of the weaknesses of his position, and of the vulnerability of his empire. Although skilled diplomacy could keep his enemies at each other's throats for the time being, the solution, as he saw it, was strength in the form of arms and armies to ensure Byzantium's long-term survival. But where was an army to be found?

Part 2

The First and Second Crusades

The First and Second Crusades

The Background to the First Crusade

When the request for aid in the struggle against the Infidel reached Rome, it was not dismissed out of hand. The Muslim conquest of Iberia, and their forays across the Pyrenees had proved a thorn in the side of the West. Numerous campaigns had been launched against them – some had even involved the Byzantines working alongside western Europeans. Rome itself was aware of the threat that Islamic forces could present – it had been sacked by them previously. With their command of the Mediterranean, Muslims were able to establish bases in Provence and Southern Italy from which they could strike at will. Tales from pilgrims returning from the Holy Land told of the desperate conditions out there. Islamic aggression appeared a threat at home and abroad.

Already in the western theatre of conflict, the Pope had encouraged French and Italian nobles to co-operate in order to come to the aid of beleaguered, Christian Spain. From 1063 expeditions were launched, often to little effect. The *Reconquista* – as the attempt to reclaim Spain from the Moors was called – was to take the better part of 800 years to achieve its aim, from its start at the Battle of Covadonga in 718 to the fall of Granada, the last Iberian Arab state, in 1492.

In 1095, however, a reclaimed Spain was centuries away. At the great council at Piacenza, Pope Urban II, amongst his other duties, received ambassadors from the Emperor Alexius. What messages they delivered are unknown. Alexius was making some headway in his fight against the Muslims and it is probable that he used a combination of his successes, and the cost to the West should he fail, as a lever to try to extract help from the Pope. The model was there in Spain, haphazard as it was, for uniting Christian forces against unbelievers. To Urban II, many personal reasons must have sprung to mind. What greater achievement could mark his papacy than a colossal campaign to free the sacred sites of the Holy Land? What effect might western involvement have on the possibilities of rapprochement with that 'dissident' eastern half of the Church? Regardless of the details, the idea for the Crusade – the taking up of arms against Christ's opponents, the great unifying cause in a Christendom split by petty disagreements and squabbles – took root in his mind between Piacenza and the first official announcement, in Clermont in France. Clermont was to be a council concerned with other clerical matters. Alongside the launch of the crusades, the Truce of God – a policy seeking to promote peace between

Christian leaders in Europe – was strongly advocated. But it was to be remembered as the start of the Crusades.

The First Crusade

On Tuesday, 27 November 1095, before a rapt and huge crowd outside the city of Clermont, Pope Urban II announced the call to arms. His speech, legend has it, was interrupted by shouts of '*Deus lo volt!*' (God wills it!). Spontaneously (or so it appeared), both rich and poor present offered to go in an enormous out-pouring of emotion. Despite the popular reception of his plan, there was a problem – Urban had not signed up any leading members of the nobility to his cause. He had an experienced and capable cleric, the Bishop of Le Puy, to take charge on behalf of the Church, but who were the men who would organise and lead the armies?

Yet this issue was quickly resolved. Beside the noble intent to fight for Christ, the spiritual pull of the call to arms, a more prosaic, more secular reason encouraged young nobles to go should the thought of rewards in the hereafter prove insufficient: primogeniture. On the death of a male member of the nobility his property and wealth would, in most of Europe, pass to the eldest son. This meant that after exhausting that pool of fighting men who were motivated by faith, or by the desire for battle and for glory, there were many ambitious young men who saw the opportunity of making their fortune under the excuse of doing good. Living in an age without newspapers and television, their prime source of information about the Holy Land was the Bible. *The Land of Milk and Honey* must have resounded in the minds of many of them. What contact they had had with Islam was enough to indicate that this was a rich and sophisticated civilisation, and the chance to take the fight to Islamic shores, after years of suffering Muslim raids, must have appealed. Life was hard enough at home for many of them. Could the East be any worse?

Rapidly, nobles came forward to sign up for the fight. Chief among them were Raymond, Count of Toulouse, and Stephen, Count of Blois; two Roberts (the Duke of Normandy and the Count of Flanders); Bohemond of Taranto and his nephew Tancred; and the brothers Baldwin, Eustace and Godfrey from Lorraine. Meanwhile more volunteers poured forth from among the poorer members of society. While Urban had instructed his bishops to preach the message, certain members of the Church went further than he would have anticipated. Indigent, wandering zealots, like Peter the Hermit, moved through towns and villages whipping up a frenzy with their preaching. The commoners were spellbound. The various spontaneous movements inspired by these preachers became known as the People's Crusade. The official Crusade was still in preparation when two huge rabbles, the first led by a Walter the Penniless, the second by Peter, set off for Constantinople. The lack of professional leadership soon became apparent. Supplies for the journey had been the last things on their minds and, as they marched through Hungary and Bulgaria, they were forced to relieve the inhabitants of what they needed. After suffering the depredations of Walter's followers, towns and villages barely had time to recover before Peter's even larger crowd appeared in their wake. From the point of view of these masses of impoverished people, driven by a fanatical desire to fight for God, farms, herds of sheep or cattle that appeared in their path must have appeared providential. The thoughts of the farmers or shepherds might have been somewhat less Christian. Infamously, it is reported that, at one stage on their journey, an argument over a pair of shoes in Hungary led to a conflict resulting in thousands of deaths.

What Alexius made of this rude army when the two forces reached Constantinople is not known. It could hardly have been what he had been expecting, much less what he had been hoping for. After spending some time in the capital – where they helped themselves to whatever came to hand, even the lead from church roofs – they crossed the Bosphorus. Despite what must have been a sense of hopelessness on Alexius' part, he must have been pleased to see them go. The absence of informed leadership, general order, any kind of clear intent and, presumably, much ability to communicate with those they met led to unsurprising results. In Asia Minor they proceeded to wreak havoc on anything and anyone unfortunate enough to lie in their path: Muslims, Christians, young and old, men and women. Most were butchered, their belongings taken and some of these sold when the opportunity or need arose (Greek sailors in coastal ports are supposed to have done well out of this trade). The local Turkish ruler soon reacted to this unholy force. First a sizeable group who had taken over the castle of Xerigordon were besieged, reduced through thirst to drinking the blood of their mounts and then their own urine, and then forced to either renounce their faith or embrace death. Those who converted to Islam were then to spend the rest of their lives as slaves.

The rest of the rag-tag army was caught out outside the town of Civetot. A minority managed to escape; a few were captured alive as slaves. The vast majority were slain. Peter had returned to Constantinople a little while before. Having been instrumental in leading tens of thousands to their deaths, and probably a little puzzled by their lack of success, he now sat back and awaited reinforcements.

As their preparations reached completion, the separate armies of the First Crusade made their way towards the East, each under separate command. Arriving at Constantinople, they experienced the same cultural queasiness that barbarians traditionally have at the courts of higher civilisations. The average soldier must have found it difficult to square his impoverished army journey with the fabulous wealth on display belonging to these people he had been called upon to 'help out' in their struggle with the infidel. And gratitude must have been the one commodity in short supply among the Byzantines, after their earlier visitors. The western leaders, however, were impressed and for the main part won over by Alexius and his generous gifts — gifts that sweetened the bitter pill of swearing an oath of allegiance to a foreign power. With a complement of Byzantines, the various forces and their leaders moved across the Bosphorus.

Their first act was to attempt to take the town of Nicaea. Here was their first battle against the enemy. Troops sent by the local Sultan to relieve the siege fought a pitched battle with the Crusaders who put up a resistance that the Turks would not have expected after their previous encounter with Peter the Hermit's men. The Turks, in the end, fled. The Christians, despite heavy losses, were jubilant. The inhabitants of Nicaea, had they been in any doubt as to who were the victors, had their hopes swiftly dashed by a rain of severed Turkish heads — hurled over the walls by the rejoicing Crusaders. When it became clear that the Emperor was bringing up support, the town bowed to the inevitable. In June 1097, Nicaea was surrendered to the Crusaders, who, in turn, presented it to Alexius. The Christian troops were no doubt displeased at the lost opportunity to pillage. Their leaders received gold; they had to be content with an extra meal.

While passing Dorylaeum, the first major test of the Crusaders' mettle occurred: a sizeable force of Turks ambushed them. The fact that these Christians were of a very different sort to the disorganised force of peasants led by Peter the Hermit had still not sunk in. The Turkish forces still expected an easy victory. As it was, the Crusaders bravely held their ground, before breaking the Turkish attack.

They continued towards the south-east. Harried sporadically as it passed through the Taurus Mountains – losing many men on the march – the army finally arrived at the outskirts of the great city of Antioch. Part of the army, under Baldwin of Boulogne, had left before this. How Baldwin justified his parting from the main army is unknown. Whatever his excuse, he gradually moved south-east towards the Armenian city of Edessa as the rest of the Crusaders moved southwest with the aim of taking Antioch. The Armenians of Edessa were a people displaced by Turkish forces from their homeland to the north-east. Now they existed as a Byzantine client state, a buffer between the Byzantine littoral and the Arabic interior. The support the Armenians received from Constantinople was essential to their continued survival but they resented being used nonetheless. The differences between Armenian and Orthodox practices and beliefs became another source of tension. But the Christians from the West had yet to sully their reputation in Armenian eyes. Baldwin's appearance was thus taken very favourably and, from the leader of a potential mercenary force against the Emir of Mosul – who was rumoured to be gathering an army to relieve Antioch that would destroy Edessa in passing – he soon rose to become first co-regent and then sole leader. Striking out on his own had proven advantageous to Baldwin, clearly a man of some ambition.

At Antioch, in October preparations had been made for the siege. The city's massive walls made it apparent that it would not fall easily. The success that the Crusaders had experienced so far had not prepared them for the slow siege that was to ensue. Days turned into weeks, and then into months. The army grew steadily more and more despondent. The news of Baldwin's easy success that filtered back to them was not necessarily – in the light of his decision to set off independently – something that would have cheered them.

More and more seemed to go against them. Supplies for the army were initially gathered from the lands around the city. As time went on, they were forced to forage further and further afield. Where was the support Alexius had promised? The hoped-for supplies failed to appear. The support from the ships of mercantile Italian cities such as Genoa, now that a section of the Holy Land coast was free of Muslim con-

trol, likewise failed to appear. Antioch itself had a substantial Christian population – the besiegers must
have expected some contribution from these natives
towards their 'liberation'. The divisive nature of sec-
tarian Christianity worked against the Crusaders here.
In Edessa, the Armenians welcomed Baldwin precisely
because he wasn't Orthodox. Here, the Syrian
Christians had no desire to place themselves under
either Orthodox or Catholic hegemony. Their estima-
tion that their Turkish masters were probably the ones
under whom they would enjoy the greater religious
freedom was probably an astute one. To the Crusaders
this must have seemed somewhere between treachery
and apostasy. Initially with these expectations of support in the air, the Crusaders were unwilling to press
the conflict until at least some of them materialised.
News of this quickly got back to Yaghi-Siyan, the
Governor of Antioch. Encouraged, he authorised
night sorties on Crusader encampments, more for
purposes of reducing morale than for any real military
gain. The city itself was safeguarded by the skills and
technologies of previous Byzantine regimes whose
experience of withstanding aggressors had made them
past masters of the art.

With winter, food became scarce. The weather
worsened as it grew colder and the rain appeared to
be unceasing. There was even an earthquake. To keep
the good Christians of the Orthodox persuasion in
order, the Turks had their most senior churchman in

the city swinging in a cage from the outer walls. There was the occasional improvement – one of the few bits of good news was the establishment of a chain of supply of food from Cyprus – and the fact that each new Islamic force that appeared on the scene to relieve the siege was driven back in disarray gave them some encouragement. Spring of 1098 saw an improvement in the weather. Some support from Constantinople would turn up in the occasional trading ship from Europe that had stopped off on the way to the Holy Land, still carrying pilgrims. Requests for more help continued to be sent back to the Emperor via these travellers. It was not long, however, before disillusioned Crusaders themselves were accompanying these requests, on their way back to Europe. By the time Alexius himself finally set off with a force to aid them, he encountered a cheerless Stephen of Blois on the road, leading a force of despondent Frenchmen whose tale that all was lost managed to convince the Emperor to turn back. It was, ironically, at this point that a breakthrough was made. Bohemond had been cultivating traitors within and finally one of them paid off. On 3 June 1098, the great outer walls of Antioch were breached and the Crusaders broke through, massacring every Muslim they found. The homes of Muslim and Christian alike were looted as the Crusaders repaid the latter for the lack of Christian solidarity.

Unfortunately the inner citadel of the city still held

out and, for its defenders, the killing of their fellow townsfolk was a fairly convincing argument in favour of continued resistance. This was not the only problem the Crusaders were to face. By this time, a sizeable force of Turks had arrived under Kerbogha of Mosul with the aim of relieving the siege. News of its approach had steeled the resolve of the citadel's inhabitants. The westerners suddenly found themselves caught like rats in a looted city, the corpses of their victims rotting in the ever-increasing summer heat. Their situation seemed hopeless, with enemies before and behind them. Then their fortunes began to change once more – this time for the better. The mood of the Crusaders began to lift after a sequence of holy signs. The supposed lance that pierced Christ's side was found under St Peter's Cathedral after a peasant's visions were acted upon. Other visions contributed to the belief that a breakthrough was just around the corner. On the Turkish side, the struggle to hold together the various forces began to show. On 28 June the armies of the Crusaders rode out, temporarily abandoning the siege, and defeated their divided opponents. The desertion by part of the Turkish army caused panic to spread among the others. Rumours of visions of knights on white horses led by saints spread inspiration through the ranks as they fought. Few of the Turks survived – many of those who escaped the battlefield were caught and killed by vengeful locals.

Watching this rout from the hill inside the city, the

inhabitants of Antioch's citadel realised there and then that it was hopeless. Arrangements were made to surrender to Bohemond of Taranto. With the other senior noble of the party, Raymond, too ill to complain, Bohemond grasped the opportunity that this victory presented him – in spite of the oaths the nobles had made that by rights this city was to be handed over upon recapture to the Emperor. When they heard later of the decision by Alexius to turn back while the siege was taking place, it both confirmed the decision in their own minds not to return Antioch to the Byzantines, and reaffirmed all the doubts they had had about them. But their anger was not reserved for the Empire alone. Stephen of Blois's reputation, already stained by his decision to leave, was tattered after they heard it was in part due to his actions that Alexius had decided to pull his reinforcements back. Yet even knowledge of Stephen's role in these events could not redeem Alexius in the eyes of the other Crusaders.

What was to become a persistent problem for the Europeans in the East made its first major appearance here: disease. Before too much time could be spent arguing over what would eventually happen to Antioch, an outbreak of plague or typhoid – hardly surprising with the heat and the dead – was upon them. It killed the one figure of sufficient seniority and wisdom who might have bridged the problems with Alexius: Adhemar of Monteil, the Bishop of Le

Puy, Urban's representative. The loss of the Pope's guiding hand represented a subtle blow to the stability of the leadership of the expedition at this point. Personal ambition probably lay not too deeply below the surface with each leader. The absence of an overall military commander from the West, the recent loosening of bonds with the Byzantines and now the loss of the Church's nominal leader of the campaign allowed these ambitions to manifest themselves crucially at the capture of these territories. The history of the Latin Kingdoms of the East (as these city states were later referred to) is ultimately one of divide and rule. The argument can never be resolved as to whether a single political force backed by a religious consensus could have held these territories more effectively yet the suspicion is obviously there. As it was, any sorrow over the loss of such an able man as Adhemar was felt more among the rank-and-file. The leadership, after Baldwin's capture of Edessa and Bohemond's move on Antioch, were out for what they could get.

Celebrations eventually gave way to the realisation that the job wasn't finished. In November 1098, the army set off again, with their sights on the even greater treasure of Jerusalem. They moved south, parallel to the Levantine coast. First they took the fortified town of Maarat. In the process, tensions between Bohemond and Raymond flared up – one presumes that Bohemond's sly grab at Antioch rankled the other commander. After the town was taken, and despite his promise to accompany the army to Jerusalem (in return for which Raymond had accepted Antioch was his), Bohemond stormed back in dudgeon to his new city to the north. Representatives of the army pressed Raymond to accept overall leadership. The other nobles had their doubts assuaged by payment. Maarat was left to burn as the army marched south, Raymond in command.

Ironically, by the time they arrived at Jerusalem they were to find that a change of ownership had taken place. The Fatamids, taking advantage of the Turkish problems in the north with the Christians, had come in force out of Egypt and re-taken the city from the Turks not long after the Crusaders had taken Antioch. Local Arab leaders in this border area between Fatamids, Turks and Christians, were not entirely convinced that these conflicts were such a bad thing. If they managed to tread a fine line of diplomacy between all sides, and kept clear of the battles, then the autonomy to be gained while their nominal rulers were preoccupied with each other was considerable. The Fatamids, who had previously watched with glee as this conflict escalated between their enemies within the faith and the Christians from without, were soon to find little to laugh about. This change of rule in Jerusalem made no difference to the Crusader forces. By the beginning of February they had taken the castle of Hosn al-Akrad. The coastal port of Tortosa was next to fall. After an unsuccessful siege of Arqa, the army moved west to follow the coast down, anxious to ensure their access to supplies that were coming in, carried to them by ships owned by Italian merchants. Now that their reputation had spread, local governors were content to pay them off rather than see their cities ravaged and burnt in the name of defending the ownership rights of their absent rulers, Turkish or Fatamid. Tripoli and Beirut both paid. Where resistance was possible the Crusaders were more and more keen to pass by, intent on Jerusalem itself. Tyre did not pay nor was it attacked as they passed. Acre paid. The inhabitants of Ramleh simply upped and left, leaving a ghost town. Ever southward they raced, the common soldiers marvelling as they passed more and more places that had previously only been known to them from tales from the Bible. Finally in June 1099, they reached Jerusalem.

As forbidding as Jerusalem's fortifications seemed, victory there proved to be more straightforward than victory at Antioch, despite many indications to the contrary. The Muslim leadership in Jerusalem had shown greater caution by driving Christians of any denomination from the city. They had substantial supplies that would see them through a lengthy siege. Morale was good since they had heard that the Fatamids were sending an army out of Egypt to destroy these foreign invaders. Yet the Crusaders now had access to the coast and, through that, to Europe via ships from Genoa and England. They had the confidence of their earlier victories and the experience of Antioch, and their final objective was in sight. Although they struggled in the Holy Land's unbearable summer heat and were debilitated by disease, although small skirmishes with Muslim forces dogged them and disagreements within the Christian camp held them back, there was, they felt, an inevitability about their victory here. The visions of priests that had played a part since Antioch continued. Saints were supposedly directing action to take place on a particular day, in a particular manner. As they liberated legendary places like Bethlehem with so little effort a sense of destiny must have overcome them. So, too, there must have been a sense among the common soldiers that after this they could perhaps go home, and there receive a reception fit for true heroes, true soldiers of Christ.

So it was that, within a couple of weeks, the siege towers were up and the Crusaders were threatening to break into the Holy City. On 15 July they did. The competition to be the first inside was fierce. Soon they were pouring into the city in great waves. Jerusalem swiftly capitulated. Raymond, in his seniority, took the surrender of the Islamic governor, Iftikhar, ransoming his life there and then and the lives of those he chose to take with him. They were among the few to survive. The army hacked and slew with an evangelical fanaticism. Even a lord like Tancred, who promised the safety of a group of Muslims hiding in a mosque, could not protect them from the fury of the soldiers. All were slain, including the Jews that had been allowed to stay – called collaborators by the Crusaders. Men, women and children were put to the sword and many were tortured beforehand. For the Jews, news of this barbarity echoed the anti-semitic attacks that had taken place in Germany at the start of the Crusaders' journey east. For the Islamic world the monstrous deeds of the Europeans here were something that would never be forgotten. Whatever deals were done after this with local Emirs or Governors, who had little love for either the Fatamids or the Turks, the acts that took place in Jerusalem that day would always be at the back of their minds.

After much debate, as had occurred in Antioch, Godfrey of Bouillon, Duke of Lower Lorraine, was elected as Defender of the Holy Sepulchre. It would perhaps have struck the Crusaders that a leader from the Church would have been more appropriate. Adhemar of Le Puy was dead, however, and the leading Greek contender, Symeon, the exiled Patriarch of Jerusalem, had also recently died. Although he was the most senior, Raymond, by his frequent attempts to assume leadership, had turned most of the other nobles against him. Godfrey was seen generally as a pious man and his assumption of the title of Defender rather than King both confirmed his piety and defused the tensions that might have arisen among so many at the presumption of kingship in the city of Christ. Once this appointment was made, and the corpses removed from the city, news of the long-expected force from the dispossessed Fatamids reached the Christians' ears – but they were obviously too late. This mighty army, lead by the Fatamid vizier, Al-Afdal, was caught by surprise outside of Ascalon on the way to relieve Jerusalem, and there slaughtered. Al-Afdal escaped with his tail between his legs, retreating to Egypt with a handful of men. The rest were scattered or killed, driven into the desert or into the sea. Much treasure was taken from the vanquished Muslim army and divided among the Christians. The Muslims of Ascalon looked on in horror at the scene that unfolded before them, doubtful of surviving a Crusade attack and petrified, after Jerusalem, of what might become of them should they surrender.

The Crusaders returned to Jerusalem. The scale of their achievement began to sink in. With the realisation that they had achieved what they had set out to do, popular feeling began to manifest itself. Many now wanted to return home because their crusading vow to liberate Jerusalem had been fulfilled. Many, however, wanted to stay, particularly those who had set out with the intention of making name and fortune for themselves in the legendary East. Robert of Normandy and Robert of Flanders gathered together their forces and began to set out for the journey back home. An unhappy Raymond accompanied them. He still held onto a dream of founding his own kingdom and yet could see little chance of realising that dream in the south, with Godfrey secure in Jerusalem.

As they headed north along the coast, they reached the Byzantine port of Lattakieh, near to Antioch. At their arrival they were alarmed to find it under attack from Bohemond (acutely aware that he was not in the Emperor's best books after keeping Antioch for himself and thus keen to secure a port to service the needs of his city) and the replacement for Adhemar, Daimbert, Archbishop of Pisa. After what must have been a spectacular display of anger by the three nobles, Daimbert – a lesser man than Adhemar in every way – called off the blockading ships that had accompanied him. Bohemond could do little but comply without the support of the Archbishop. The two Roberts returned to Europe via Constantinople to a heroic welcome. Raymond, having firmly nailed his colours to the Byzantine mast, stayed on in Lattakieh, puzzling over his next move.

The promises they had all made on taking up the cross now became pressing. Bohemond of Antioch and Baldwin of Edessa made their pilgrimage to Jerusalem. Godfrey, after the departure of so many men with the armies returning home, was keen to bolster the small army he had left to defend the lands in the south. Many of the knights who accompanied Bohemond and Baldwin were induced to stay by the offer of lands and titles. Tancred, meanwhile, had been directing a series of successful raids in Galilee, consol-idating the territories held by the westerners.

With each town taken, each fortress claimed from the Muslims, the position of the Crusaders became more secure. Local Turkish emirs began to make peace with Godfrey. Little was heard from the defeated Fatamids. Alexius, despite the various problems along the way, must have been relieved. At the very least the heat was off Constantinople. He now had the Crusaders and their military gains as a buffer against the Muslims.

After the First Crusade:
The Latin Kingdoms of the East

News of the success of the Crusade had now pene-trated Europe and first to appear in response had been the representatives of the Italian maritime states. The wealth of their cities was based exclusively on the trade that came from their fleets, and the goods that they could then sell on into Europe. While they had been able to do business with Islam, they swiftly recognised the new business opportunities that would come with their co-religionists in charge. The Crusaders would not be able to survive without sup-port from Europe. The Venetians were swiftly on the scene, offering the use of their ships and men in fur-ther battles in return for preferential treatment and bases in the Holy Land.

After the debacle at Lattakieh, Daimbert arrived in Jerusalem, keen to make both his mark and his fortune. He assumed the role of Patriarch of Jerusalem, guaranteeing that the Church there was to be firmly under the yoke of Rome rather than Constantinople. At this point fate intervened. Godfrey was struck down with a disease that eventually was to prove fatal. Loyalties were split along family lines when it came down to the question of succession. Tancred was behind his uncle Bohemond while Baldwin justified his rights by fraternal ties. Raymond – a man who had had as much claim to leadership of the campaign as any – had failed to make any territory his own and, after Lattakieh, had put himself out of contention by returning to Constantinople to make the most of his relationship with the Emperor. While Bohemond's claim was strong, he managed to rule himself out after being captured by the Turks in a conflict in the north. Imprisoned in a cell in a remote mountain castle in Asia Minor his career plans were very much on hold. Daimbert allied himself with Tancred initially but quickly came to accept the realities of the situation. Baldwin, after winning much popular support from Bohemond's army when he interceded to ensure Antioch's protection after the latter's capture, rode to Jerusalem and was proclaimed King on 11 November 1100. Daimbert conducted the official ceremony that was to follow.

Baldwin proved to be an exemplary, as well as fortunate, choice. He recognised that the key to holding on to the conquests was solidarity among the leaders of the Crusade and the establishment of defendable kingdoms. Throughout his reign he proved his talents as a leader time and again by his subtle and skilled negotiations with both allies and enemies. The two senior leaders, Bohemond and Raymond, were, in one way or another, sidelined. The others never seriously challenged Baldwin's position as overlord.

The political state of the area at the opening of the 12th century was complex. Alexius had won back much of western Asia Minor and many of the coastal areas of the south through his own skilful manoeu-vrings and by taking advantage of the fact that many of his opponents were preoccupied with the Franks. (Franks was a term that was used by the Muslims to describe all the newcomers from Europe.) To his east were his old Muslim enemies, the Seldjuks of Rum, who were now as concerned with their neighbouring fellow-Muslims, the Danishmends, and the Norman-controlled Principality of Antioch (and to a lesser extent the County of Edessa) as they were with the Emperor. Edessa itself was in a nightmarish position. With the exception of the Normans to the west, who were never the most reliable of allies, it was sur-rounded on every other side by Muslim forces: Rum to the north-west, the Danishmends to the north, the Ortoqids to the east and several semi-independent Muslim rulers to the south. It was a territory that was impossible to defend adequately: it was the fortresses of Edessa that were held, not the countryside. Edessa was also, to a great extent, Armenian, and the Armenian people were less comfortable with foreign rule than the melting-pot communities of the coast. It lacked the riches of a great city such as Antioch, the mercantile opportunities of the ports and, with an impoverished peasantry who scratched a poor living from the land when they were not being put to the sword by invaders, there was little chance of generating great revenue through taxes. Baldwin's cousin and the man who was to inherit Edessa from him, another Baldwin, this time originally of Le Bourg, became notorious for raising a substantial sum to pay his army by blackmailing his father-in-law, Gabriel. Local custom dictated beards — when Baldwin II threatened to shave his off Gabriel stumped up 30,000 bezants to save the shame it would bring on him and their family by association.

Between these two Christian states and the Kingdom of Jerusalem lay independent Islamic cities, whose loyalties had traditionally been obtained by force by either the Fatamids in Egypt or the Abbasids of the Middle East, and bandit country. Baldwin had three strategic aims: to protect his northern borders by removing the intervening Muslim rulers between the Latin lands; to protect his western flank by control of the coastal cities of the Levant (and hence to guarantee supplies of materials and men arriving from

Europe); and to extend the southern borders until he reached the Red Sea, preventing the Fatamids from providing easy support to other Muslims. By the time of his death in 1119, Baldwin had achieved each of these aims. He nearly lost his life in numerous confrontations with the enemy, sometimes escaping by the skin of his teeth. He fought enemies within as well as without. Daimbert's greed saw him exiled once and then, after making a show of contrition and returning, for a second, final time. Each battle won, each city successfully besieged made the Latin Kingdom of Jerusalem's long-term survival more likely. Within the kingdom Baldwin encouraged mixing between the differing groups, to the extent of allowing marriage between Christians and Muslims. Most importantly, in terms of conflict, he withstood the forces of Fatamid Egypt. Their defeat for the third time in battle at Ramleh appeared to be final. Against Baldwin's greatness, the others often seemed bit-players in an enormous farce.

To win Tancred over to the idea of Baldwin's kingship, the latter had found it necessary to offer his rival the position of regent of Antioch, a role to be relinquished when Bohemond was released. Tancred threw a few tantrums before coming to the realisation that this position might not turn out to be so temporary after all. It removed the most troublesome of Baldwin's allies to a convenient distance and yet it made use of him. Tancred was as able as he was difficult. Before Bohemond's capture he had adroitly taken much of Galilee to the north of Jerusalem. Giving him Antioch was both a reward and a burden. Relations between the Byzantines and the Normans had been tricky since way before the Crusades. The Normans had taken Byzantine land in southern Italy; they had fought against the Empire in Greece. It was no accident that a previous Emperor had chosen to replace his personal bodyguard of Normans with one comprised of Anglo-Saxon exiles who had fled England after William the Conqueror had taken control. Alexius would never forgive Bohemond for his refusal to relinquish Antioch and ensuring the persistence of enmity between the two by ensuring Antioch remained out of the former's hands might have seemed advantageous to a King of Jerusalem who could have expected interference from both.

In 1101 more crusaders set out from Europe, heartened by the success of the First Crusade and keen to play a part. Some were old hands. Stephen of Blois was among them, perhaps keen to make up for his flight from the siege of Antioch. At Constantinople they met both the Emperor and Raymond. In all, three such armies came over into Asia Minor and each was annihilated in turn by the Turks, whose self-confidence grew with each inflicted calamity. For Raymond, who had joined them from Constantinople, the repeated disaster that overcame each army must have been close to the final straw. As dejected as he may have felt, nothing prepared him for the reception that he was to receive when he arrived with the other surviving nobility from the new campaigns at Antioch. The grand welcome extended even to the 'cowardly' Stephen of Blois vanished at Raymond's appearance. Tancred's lieutenant, the delightfully named Bernard the Stranger, stepped forward and arrested him, ostensibly on account of his behaviour in one of these later crusading disasters. There was popular indignation over the arrest, but Tancred managed to get an oath from Raymond to the effect that he would abandon any interest in that area. Raymond was set free, and promptly left with a force in a southern direction.

Tancred then turned to the task that had defeated his uncle – the capture of the port of Lattakieh. He succeeded after a long siege. Alexius was furious. Tancred at this point was not the most popular of figures and, as an inevitable consequence of his success, an international whip-round ensued to free Bohemond. When Bohemond was finally released in 1103, Tancred was one of the few who hadn't offered to contribute to the fund. Bohemond thanked him for his stewardship of Antioch and assumed rule. It was fortunate for Tancred that very soon afterwards, Baldwin II was captured, and Tancred neatly stepped into his shoes, again on the basis that it was a temporary position. The response of Baldwin II, whose growing distrust of Tancred had led him to be one of the prime instigators of the ransoming of Bohemond, could not have been sweet. Who was likely to ransom him? When an opportunity arrived in the shape of a Seldjuk princess captured by Tancred, the offer of an exchange of Baldwin for the Seldjuk by the Turks – an act strongly encouraged by Baldwin of Jerusalem – was turned down quietly. The two Norman leaders opted for hard currency instead of a ransomed noble.

With increased Turkish pressure on Antioch, Alexius decided it was time to take action and launched a successful recovery of much of Lattakieh. Bohemond realised that he was in an increasingly difficult situation. The only support he could envisage would be from Europe and so he set off to Rome with the aim of convincing Urban II's successor, the vastly-inferior Pope Paschal, that the Byzantines were more of a threat to them than the Turks. This he managed to do. With Papal backing he launched an attack on the Empire, an act that was to forever poison the relationship between the two halves of the Church. In the end he was defeated by Alexius, humiliated by having to swear fealty to the latter and retired to his provinces in Italy. He died there, never having returned to Antioch which was now held, as was Edessa, by Tancred.

But Bohemond was to outlive Raymond. After being turfed out of Antioch, Raymond persisted with his plans for his own little kingdom. He managed to take Tortosa on the Levantine coast and to win some spectacular battles against the Muslims. A hero to his own troops, he died some months after receiving burns in an unsuccessful siege of Tripoli, having gone some way toward restoring his dignity. His followers there elected his cousin, William-Jordan of Cerdagne, as his successor, an inheritance that was to be disputed when Raymond's illegitimate son, Bertrand the Bastard, turned up from France. As the two men captured towns and cities in the Levant ill-feeling intensified between them. William-Jordan sought Tancred as a supporter and Bertrand, Baldwin. Things reached a head and Baldwin was forced to divide the conquered land between them, to be unified under whoever outlived the other. When William-Jordan, in the security of his own camp, suffered one of those inexplicable deaths under friendly fire not long after, a new County of Tripoli, perched on the coast between Antioch and Jerusalem, arose to join the other three kingdoms.

By this point Baldwin II had been ransomed and, after a struggle, had persuaded Tancred to give back Edessa. The enmity between the two was best illustrated by the battle between the Muslim forces of Jawali and Ridwan in 1108. Tancred and Baldwin both took part as allies – on opposing sides. Later, at the same conference called to sort out William-Jordan and Bertrand, Baldwin of Jerusalem had similarly to knock the heads of Tancred and Baldwin II together.

By 1111, Alexius in turn had had his fill of Tancred. He sent his envoys to the east to meet with the Caliph of Baghdad in an attempt to convince him to move on

Tancred's principality. Alexius's men were not the first to come to Baghdad with this suggestion. When they arrived they found Muslims there from Aleppo urging the same course. When news of Alexius's mission leaked out, he was to hear that the rabble had proclaimed him a greater Muslim than the unwilling Caliph.

A new force entered Muslim politics at this time, organised by a man known as Hassan-I-Sabah. In time, each leader of this cult became known as the Old Man of the Mountains. This cult, the Assassins, were members of the Ismaili sect, and directed their energies as a consequence of their religious beliefs against their fellow-Muslims the Abbasids in the east, and their masters there, the Seldjuk Turks (who were a separate dynasty from the Seldjuks in Asia Minor). All Sunni Muslims learnt to fear them and the Crusaders soon did so too. To some degree the Europeans had taught the Muslims the secular benefits of religious fanaticism by their conquests. The Muslims, in turn, came back with the first real terrorists. Their adherents were anonymous, rumoured to be on drugs, and cared little for their earthly fate once their victim was murdered. Their reputation was more effective than their acts. Fear of a sudden unexpected attack in the middle of a crowded marketplace or square notched up the paranoia levels among several leaders.

A generation now began to pass away. Tancred was taken by disease in 1112. In 1118 Alexius died. The next year saw the death of Baldwin of Jerusalem. He had almost become a legend by this time, an Alfred the Great to his subjects – the most popular leader among the Latins in the Holy Land. The throne passed to his cousin, Baldwin of Edessa. Almost immediately Baldwin's mettle was tested by an attempt against the Franks by the Ortoqids. The Crusaders lost men in a number of battles, suffering particularly when most of Antioch's army was massacred at what became known as the Field of Blood, but Baldwin was to steer them through these troubles with most of their territories left intact, thus confirming his primacy among rulers of the Latin Kingdoms.

Support from Europe now came in a different form. From the years before the First Crusade an order called the Hospitallers had been formed to support pilgrims on their way to the Holy Land. Soon after Baldwin's ascension, the idea arose to turn this order into something more. Moving from passive support to an active role, the Hospitallers became a Military Order, an organisation of knights dedicated to ensuring the continued success of the Crusades. At the same time another order, the Knights of the Temple, formed. The idea spread. In the coming decades more and more orders were formed, in the Holy Land and in Europe, merging religious dedication and knightly valour. None were to prove as successful, or in the end as wealthy, as these first two orders. Although the numbers of knights they provided for action in the East were never huge, when situations grew tight they were often to provide an invaluable additional force, and a self-financing one at that. They were to also prove an almost unparalleled source of dissension in the latter years of the Latin Kingdoms.

Control of Edessa passed to Joscelin of Courtenay, a relative of Baldwin. The Franks, after the successful resistance against the Ortoqids, were soon back in trouble again. Joscelin was captured in 1123 and before long Baldwin himself had joined him. An undercover force of Armenians miraculously sprang them from prison before the Muslims could make anything of holding two of the three most senior Christian rulers in the region.

The Venetians were brought in with an attempt to take Tyre, an island fortress that had been joined to the coast by a strip of land by Alexander the Great when he captured it more than a thousand years before. After a long siege it fell, the first important gain made by the Christians in years. Bohemond's young son, Bohemond II, came out from Italy to claim his Principality of Antioch. The handsome and promising youth's career was to be cut short – by 1130 his severed head was an embalmed gift in the palace of the Caliph of Baghdad. The final members of the old guard passed with the long, lingering death of Baldwin II in 1131 and that of Joscelin of Edessa the same year from wounds gained in a siege when one of his own tunnels collapsed under him.

For thirty years the Latin Kingdoms had endured. Despite the potentially overwhelming forces surrounding them, forceful and generally unified leadership had held firm against opponents generally in disarray. Attachments to the West were still strong – more and more pilgrims visited. Trade was facilitated through the capture of more coastal towns and closer links with Genoa and Venice, although the deals struck with the two Italian city-states began to see more and more of the profits that might have bolstered the East pass into their hands. Of the new organisations the Military Orders were bringing additional fighting power and tightening the connections with Europe: the Assassins divided the Muslims further.

What the forces of Islam needed was a leader they could get behind, a heroic figure who could unite them. The first step was to realise that their true enemies were not each other. The pendulum was to swing back towards Islam over the next few years. The Crusaders had already reached their peak in some respects, although they did not recognise it at the time. The novelty of the appeal of the original Crusade became a difficult attraction to re-create. Winning back Jerusalem was an easier thing to sell to the West than holding it and, as it gradually became apparent that the support of Europe was to be a constant requirement, the new Latin rulers of the East must have wondered for how long that support could be relied upon.

The Second Crusade

For the Latin Kingdoms, the Second Crusade should have been a marvellous shot in the arm. In execution, it was to prove one administered to the foot. By 1145, news reached the Pope, Eugenius III, that the County of Edessa had fallen. After nearly fifty years the joyous news of the First Crusade had settled down into a comfortable acceptance of Christianity's pre-eminence there. Church bells had rung throughout Europe's countryside at the news of Jerusalem's recapture. The reports of Edessa's recapture by the Muslims was used to issue a new call to arms by Eugenius, and this caught the imaginations of many of the nobility of Western Europe. There was the chance for younger sons passed over in succession to win lands in the Levant, and the opportunity to match the heroic deeds of fathers or uncles, grandfathers or great uncles who had gone across the Mediterranean to fight in that most laudable of contests. Both ideas were attractive.

Eugenius chose as leader of the Crusade, Louis VII of France. The problems associated with a split leadership were lessons that had been learnt. What Eugenius did not count on was the enthusiasm of St Bernard of Clairvaux, the pre-eminent churchman of the time, who carried the call into Germany, infecting the king there, Conrad, with his enthusiasm. Two huge armies set off in 1147 under the two kings. Conrad arrived first in Constantinople, having trailed chaos in the wake of his army on the way. There was an incident in Greece where a juggler trying to earn an honest crust was accused by German soldiers of witchcraft and the usual devastation followed. Louis followed soon afterwards. Tensions between the French and Germans were strong.

A useful ally could have been King Roger II of Sicily, a Norman lord who, in addition to Sicily, owned much of southern Italy. However, Eugenius had fallen out with Roger and thus the benefits of a possible third army were lost. Roger had experience in fighting the Muslims, having taken Malta and after several attempts, Tripoli, establishing a Norman colony on the North African coast. He also had a substantial sea-force. Unfortunately Roger had ruffled feathers by his claims both to Antioch – as Bohemond's nearest male heir – and to Jerusalem after his mother's short second marriage to Baldwin I (where a contract had been signed promising him the succession).

Conrad's army left for Asia Minor. Ignoring the Byzantine Emperor Manuel's suggestion that they travel as far as possible through his territory on the way to the Holy Land, the over-confident Germans set off straight into Seldjuk country. They were not prepared with sufficient supplies for the journey, and were certainly not prepared for the reception they would receive. At the first opportunity to obtain water, thirsty, they broke formation. The knights climbed down from their horses, and without any semblance of order, stumbled towards the river before them. The Turks were waiting. They descended upon the German rabble and a tremendous slaughter ensued. Conrad survived with a fragment of the army, fleeing back along the roads to Byzantine territory. When news of the Germans' fate reached Louis he decided to take Manuel's earlier advice. His army travelled by land until a convenient point came where Louis and most of the nobility could take to the sea. The unfortunate remainder, along with the remnants of the hapless German force, finally reached Antioch after almost constant harrying by the Turks. Despite attempts to convince him to fight there, Louis carried on down to Jerusalem.

He arrived to find that Conrad, who had initially stayed in Constantinople to recuperate, had beaten him to it – sensibly travelling by sea from Manuel's capital direct to Acre. By now Manuel's reputation was in tatters among the new Crusaders. As their predecessors had before, everything that went wrong they blamed upon the Byzantines. The final straw was Manuel's treaty with the Seldjuk Turks of Asia Minor, the same forces who had slaughtered so many of their fellow countrymen. The fact that he was forced into it, urgently needing to free up his forces to fight in Greece against Roger of Sicily (who had taken the opportunity of the distractions in Asia Minor to invade) was of no concern. This act of diplomacy confirmed the prejudices the westerners held.

The arrival in Jerusalem, however, was a cause for celebration among the inhabitants of that city. Queen Melisende with her teenage son, King Baldwin III, ruled the city jointly. Melisende was the daughter of Baldwin II and had ruled with her son since the death of her husband, Fulk of Anjou, in 1143. Thoughts of re-conquering Edessa fell by the wayside. It was decided instead to launch an attack on the nearest rich Muslim capital, Damascus. This was not to prove the wisest of moves.

One candidate for the role of the heroic figurehead that Islam had been waiting for had appeared some few decades before. Imad ad-din Zangi ibn aq Sonqur, commonly referred to as Zangi, was the son of the governor of Aleppo. Through skilful manoeuvring, and the support of the Seldjuks, he extended his control from Mosul to an ever-increasing area of Syria. It was Zangi who had conquered Edessa – an act that catapulted him to fame in the Islamic world. He saw himself as the man to rid Islam of the Franks and, when not fighting them directly, took on those Muslims who chose to ally themselves with the Christians. The success of Edessa was never followed up. Zangi had wanted to press on and take control of Damascus, an act that would have made him a perpetual thorn in the Latin Kingdom's side. It was not to be. In 1146 a eunuch murdered him in his sleep, in the middle of a campaign, laying siege to the stronghold of a rebellious Arab prince.

The Franks must have breathed a sigh of collective relief. Their relief was short-lived. Zangi's son Nur ed-Din proved to be made of the same sort of stuff as his father and had the same intent – to send the Franks, those that he did not put to the sword, scurrying back to Europe. Nur ed-Din had the same ambition to take Damascus, a town ruled by the Emir Unur. Unur, eager to remain independent, was in a difficult position. Caught between the Franks and Nur ed-Din he cultivated a good relationship with the former, suspecting that they represented less of a threat to him.

When the mighty combined force of Louis and Conrad and the Latin Kingdoms appeared outside Damascus, with its soldiers confidently walking beneath the town's orchards and through the gardens on the outskirts of the city, Unur was faced with a terrible decision. Should he call for help from Nur ed-Din? While he could he drew in local reinforcements and fortified the city. A few skirmishes took place. The Franks made more than their fair share of mistakes. However, it soon became clear that, in the end, Unur would not be able to resist their tremendous advantage of numbers. Forced by circumstance, he entered into discussions with Nur ed-Din. When news of these talks reached the ears of the Latins, the folly of what they had embarked on became clear. News of the army Nur ed-Din was gathering began to come through. While they were confident of their ability to take Damascus on its own, Nur ed-Din's entry into the fray risked not only the chance of taking Damascus but also a complete defeat in the shape of the establishment of a hostile and powerful enemy immediately on their borders. Or so the threat appeared to the native, Christian nobles. Louis and Conrad, on the other hand, couldn't see the problem. Muslims were Muslims – so why the sudden change of heart? As time went on, the Latins' nerves failed. They convinced Louis and Conrad to retreat. Damascus was safe from both for the time being, and the Second Crusade was effectively over.

Conrad returned to Europe. Any responsibility for the failure of the Crusade he might have laid at Constantinople's door was forgotten. His hatred of Roger of Sicily was paramount, and any foe of Roger's (the conflict between the Normans and Byzantines continued) was a friend of his. Louis hung on in the East for a while, uncertain as to what he should do. Eventually he too returned home to Europe. The blame for the failure of the Crusade was laid by Louis firmly at Manuel's door. Once back in France he agitated against Manuel but, without Conrad's support, a new crusade (this time against Constantinople) was out of the question, however much the Roman Church might have supported it. Neither Conrad nor Louis can have had tremendous respect for the leaders of Outremer (the medieval term for the Crusader states) after the debacle at Damascus. The new crusaders had

been shocked by what they found in the East: westerners adopting eastern dress, fraternising with infidels.
Naively, they had expected a similar society to the one
they knew in Europe. What they found was a melting-
pot of West and East, a society where merchants from
Genoa and Venice mixed with their Arabic counter-
parts, a society where the members of numerous
heretical Christian cults lived alongside those adherents to the true faith of Rome. In fifty years generations had grown up in the East whose idea of Europe
was based on what they heard from pilgrims, and the
tales their parents and grandparents had told. The new
Crusaders were labouring under a tremendous misap-
prehension. They had come to take part in a Holy War
but, to the people they were trying to save, it was an
almost entirely political affair.

The Latin Kingdoms would have to wait years
before more help would be forthcoming from Europe
as a consequence. Nur ed-Din would consolidate his
power. And soon was to come a man who would
assume an even more heroic role in Islamic eyes, the
greatest figure to take the field against the foreign
invaders – Saladin.

The Crusades to the Middle East
1096 – 1204

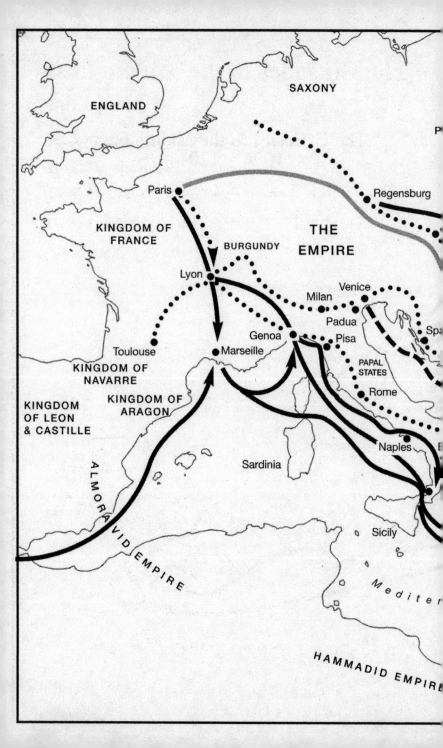

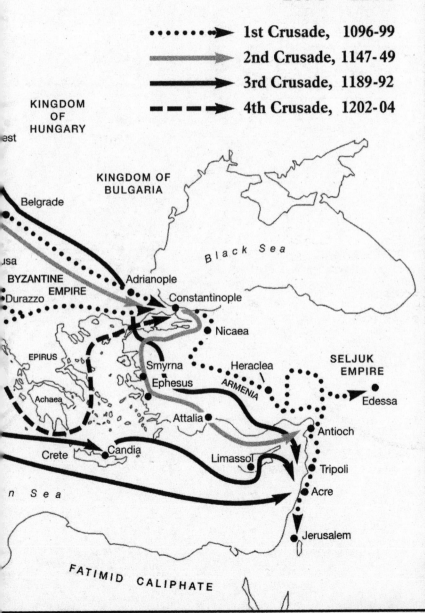

The Crusades to the Middle East, 1096 – 1204

- ••••••→ 1st Crusade, 1096-99
- ──────→ 2nd Crusade, 1147-49
- ──────→ 3rd Crusade, 1189-92
- ─ ─ ─ →4th Crusade, 1202-04

KINGDOM OF HUNGARY

est

KINGDOM OF BULGARIA

Belgrade

Black Sea

usa

BYZANTINE EMPIRE

Durazzo

Adrianople

Constantinople

Nicaea

EPIRUS

Smyrna

Heraclea

SELJUK EMPIRE

Ephesus

ARMENIA

Achaea

Edessa

Attalia

Antioch

Crete

Candia

Limassol

Tripoli

Acre

n Sea

Jerusalem

FATIMID CALIPHATE

Part 3

The Third and Fourth Crusades

The Third and Fourth Crusades

The Background to the Third Crusade

In the years following the Second Crusade, Nur ed-Din strengthened his grip on the lands surrounding the Christians. The success was not entirely one-sided. King Baldwin III, ruling now on his own, took the great southern coastal fortress of Ascalon in 1153. This was a prestigious victory and bolstered Outremer's defences against a possible attack from the Fatamid regime in Egypt, although, in truth, the Fatamid threat had shrunk through time after a succession of weak rulers. What was an entirely more pertinent yet quieter victory came the next year when the populace of Damascus received Nur ed-Din into their city and their hearts. Nur ed-Din did not press this new advantage over the Christians immediately. Other concerns were soon foremost in his mind. Earthquakes struck the region in 1156 and coping with the ensuing damage was to occupy Christian and Muslim alike.

Conflict was now to centre in the north. Reynald of Chatillon was another one of those sons of the nobility who, because of the laws of primogeniture, had decided to stay on in the East after Louis of France had left, seeking his fortune. He cunningly married his way into power in Antioch. This was not enough for him. Taking advantage of Manuel's preoccupations he again made Antioch live up to its reputation as a thorn in the Empire's side. While Manuel was occupied with the Seldjuks and, in addition, their Armenian neighbours, Reynald, in league with the Templars, formulated a plan to raid the rich, Byzantine-held island of Cyprus. Here was best illustrated the negative side of the Military Orders. While their ever-increasing roles, both as policemen guarding pilgrim routes and fortresses, and their contribution as elite warriors in battle, were of great benefit, their independent leadership could as easily work against the greater interests of the Franks as with them. Jealousies between the Orders proved as destructive.

Reynald, as an outsider in Antioch, was not particularly loved. His cunning plan to raise the funds to accomplish his mission made him despised. A leading and much respected (not to say wealthy) churchman in the city was arrested, tortured, and his still-fresh wounds anointed with honey. Reynald then had him staked to a roof until the ministrations of the local ants, flies and wasps convinced him to give up his money to the cause. With these funds Reynald set out to Cyprus and, in the process of liberating it of its wealth and potential hostages, reduced it to a state of such misery that it became the target of any pirate in the area. Baldwin was horrified and Manuel was spitting with rage. When Reynald was later captured by Muslims the rejoicing could be heard from Constantinople to Jerusalem, among peasants and nobles alike.

In 1162, Baldwin III died at the relatively young age of thirty-three. His brother Amalric, Count of Ascalon, took the throne. Meanwhile weak rule in Egypt descended into a state of near-chaos. Nur ed-Din saw an opportunity to conquer the kingdom and Amalric, at the very least, felt a requirement to ensure that it did not fall into Nur ed-Din's hands. After a game of cat-and-mouse, where Amalric would head south towards the Nile and then be dragged back by Nur ed-Din's attacks in his absence, 1167 saw armies of both sides near Cairo. The Franks were led by Amalric; the Muslims by Nur ed-Din's right-hand man, Shirkuh. With Shirkuh was his nephew, a young man by the name of Saladin. The Egyptians knew that the Franks could be bought off. Nur ed-Din, however, was out to build an empire. With Fatamid money in their purses, the Franks and their Egyptian allies presented too formidable an opponent. Shirkuh eventually withdrew. Amalric, with the threat gone, and substantially richer, followed.

Rumours of the son of the Egyptian vizier's friendship with Shirkuh, a desire for more gold and the interests of new Crusaders from the West soon brought an army back under Amalric. The vizier, Shawar, was horrified. He contacted Shirkuh and, through him, Nur ed-Din. Any idea to play the two sides off against each other in the way that Damascus had, years before, was a pipe dream. Nur ed-Din was not to make the same mistake again. Shirkuh and Saladin returned to Egypt and, grasping the opportunity fate had presented, met up with the unsuspecting vizier. In a very short time, they ended his rule of Egypt by parting his head from his shoulders. Shawar had never been that popular, and Shirkuh was canny enough to inveigle his way into the kingship, as the loyal servant of Nur ed-Din. Shirkuh did not enjoy his new position long – within months he was dead from over-keen celebration.

Whoever was blamed for this, Amalric and his barons were agreed on one thing – they were now well and truly in it, up to their necks. Amalric sent requests for a new Crusade to anybody he could think of in Europe of major standing. They were all otherwise engaged. He turned to the only possible source of aid, Manuel. In 1169, a joint force set off for Egypt – Amalric on land, the Byzantines by sea. Their attempt produced no positive result. The Franks were too cautious to attack, the Byzantines too short of supplies (a situation aggravated by the impoverished state of Cyprus) to wait. Recriminations flew between the two sides. In 1170, to cap the problems, earthquakes struck again.

Saladin inherited Egypt from Shirkuh. With Egypt added to his territories, Nur ed-Din should have moved against the Franks. In reality, however, he grew to distrust Saladin more and more. Saladin had his own problems with potential coups against him at home and the fact that Nur ed-Din was uncertain of his loyalties merely disinclined Saladin to take up arms against the Franks. Much in the same way that Alexius had viewed the County of Edessa, Saladin could not miss the benefits of having a buffer between himself and his master. His excuses were met with greater suspicion; his apologies and vows of obeisance became less and less convincing. In the end what saved him was Nur ed-Din's death in May 1174. Any cheer at this event for the Franks was dissipated by the death of Amalric, two months later.

At first both sides seemed in the same boat – rudderless. It was not obviously apparent at this point the role that Saladin would later play. For the Franks the situation was far more desperate. Amalric's only son, Baldwin, was a thirteen-year-old leper. Among them too, there was a greater degree of dissension. The Templars were increasingly following an agenda at odds with that of the Frankish barons. Amalric had received ambassadors from the Assassins in 1173 suggesting an alliance against Nur ed-Din. Their leader, Rashid ed-Din Sinan – who was the pre-eminent Old Man of the Mountains – was a cunning and dangerous opponent. As an ally he represented, at the very least, a terrorist who could act as a major irritant to the Franks' main enemy. After a very positive meeting, the ambassadors left and were promptly ambushed and slaughtered by a group of Templars. Outraged, Amalric sought to punish the ringleader of the act and was even more put out when the Templar Grand Master refused to hand him over (Amalric had to seize him by force.) The Templars pursued a far more rigid policy than most of refusing to negotiate with the enemy and, for them, the enemy was every Muslim. In this they found common cause with the new Crusaders who still pro-vided a small but steady source of fighting men. In opposition were the more pragmatic Hospitallers and most of the local barony. While Amalric was alive and the Templars and recent immigrants were without a figurehead, these tensions were controlled. Within a year of Amalric's death, the freeing of the notorious Reynald of Chatillon gave the latter group someone who would fill the desired position. Raymond of Tripoli was by then acting as Regent in Jerusalem while the young, leper prince edged towards his matu-rity. Neither of them could be expected to impose their will upon dissenters with the same force as the able and experienced Amalric.

In Asia Minor things proceeded to go very badly too for the Byzantines. After a period of détente with the Seldjuks, tensions rose. Manuel decided to try to sort them out once and for all. He sent out an army under his cousin, Andronicus. It was defeated at Niksar and its leader beheaded. He followed this with an army that displayed the full might of the Empire and it, in turn, was crushed mercilessly by the Turks at Myriocephalum in 1176. In Europe and among certain Christian factions rejoicing took place at the defeat of the traitorous Byzantines. Among the Franks of a less evangelical persuasion the removal of the Greeks as a deciding force in Asia Minor only ensured that the Seldjuks would soon be free to turn their attentions south.

The next few years saw Saladin gradually tighten the pressure on the Franks. Egypt's natural resources were considerable. It had been the breadbasket of the ancient world. Much of the considerable traffic in exotic goods by sea from India and the Far East passed through its ports on the way to Europe. Next to the Latin Kingdoms it was rich beyond compare. Without support from Europe things were only going to deteriorate for the Christians. They defeated Saladin at Montgisard in 1177 by drawing on every man they could find and ambushing the Muslims. But the tide had turned after the better part of a century of success for the Franks. Once again, nature interceded on their behalf – this time in the shape of famine. Saladin agreed to a two-year truce with the young leper king in 1180. He wasn't exactly in a rush. He used the time instead to strengthen his control over his governors, and to force peace treaties with the few independent Muslim forces, such as the Seldjuks.

Among the Franks, the extremist forces around Reynald gained power at the expense of others. Baldwin, particularly once without Raymond as Regent, could not stand against them. The few sound advisors he had were marginalised, or died. In Constantinople, Manuel himself was dying and in Jerusalem the leper-king's illness progressed.

After Manuel's death the Empire was in upheaval. One ruler followed swiftly after another. Notoriously, in 1182, part of the tensions between vying factions in the Palace erupted as a spontaneous attack by the common people on the westerners living in the capital. Most were killed — and it was a day that would not be forgotten in the West, whatever restitutions were made. What added to this crime in the eyes of the Franks was the non-aggression pact that stood between the Byzantines and Saladin.

Outside of Egypt, Saladin's empire increased. By 1183 he had moved his capital to Damascus as a more central point from which to rule. In Jerusalem the exercise of power was in the hands of Baldwin's brother-in-law, Guy. The King's leprosy had advanced to the point where he was rotting away in bed. Reynald, in a particular stroke of genius, chose this time to set out on a shipboard expedition into the Red Sea. Most of his victims there proved to be Muslim pilgrims. More odium was heaped upon the Franks in response and the few friends they had among the Muslims were lost by this act of impiety. Guy and

Baldwin fell out with each other and Baldwin reclaimed his role as king for a final few months before his death in 1185. Saladin agreed to another truce, this time for four years, and, as before, used the time to consolidate his power. Baldwin's nephew, Baldwin V, a child, was appointed King with Raymond again as Regent. The child died at nine. Guy and his wife claimed the throne after some dissent. More problems were to come from Reynald who, being instrumental in Guy's accession, now felt he could act without constraint with Guy in power – payback for his support. He would again raid Muslim merchant caravans despite the truce with Saladin.

When Saladin finally made his move it was the greatest calamity to fall upon Outremer. His army met the combined forces of the Latin Kingdoms, with Templars and Hospitallers taking part, at Hattin in 1187. The Crusaders were boxed in, desperate for water, while the surrounding Muslims jubilantly antic- ipated victory. Raymond was heard crying out 'Ah, Lord God, the war is over; we are dead men; the king- dom is finished' as the parched soldiers lay there in the night, acrid smoke from the bushes surrounding the camp, set alight by the Muslims, adding to their dis- comfort. The next morning at dawn the Muslims attacked. A tiny force escaped from the mass slaugh- ter. Many of the senior figures were caught and brought to Saladin's tent, King Guy and Reynald and the Grand Master of the Templars among them.

Forgiveness was not foremost in Saladin's mind.

All the Templars captured were given over to Sufi mystics who had followed the army – they took great delight in torturing and then killing them. Reynald, as the most hated figure in the Islamic world, did not even bother arguing for his life. The little he did manage to say before Saladin picked up his sword, walked over and despatched him straight to the next world, is unrecorded. Even after so many dead, the market was bloated with Frankish prisoners – a slave could be bought for the price of a pair of sandals.

From here the victors went on to capture most of the Kingdom of Jerusalem. Soon the territory held by the Franks was restricted to fortresses and the city of Jerusalem itself. Christians from the surrounding countryside flocked to Jerusalem and prayed for God's mercy in their time of trial. In 1187, Jerusalem fell to Saladin. More and more refugees made their way to the coast, looking for, at best, a passage out, at worst aware that the great coastal fortresses like Tyre were their last hope. South of Tripoli, the Franks had been virtually swept from the map. Jerusalem had lasted barely a century under Christian rule. Now it had fallen to the one man capable of uniting the Islamic world against the foreign invaders. Could Christian Europe take it back?

The Third Crusade

As the news of the fall of Jerusalem spread across the European continent it was met with both dismay and surprise. Regular news of the turbulent conditions of the East had not led people in Europe to expect that things really were this bad. The instant response that the Latin Christians might have hoped for was unlikely since Crusades were, since the Second Crusade, now the sport of kings. As such, the leading participants of the Third Crusade would need to put their own affairs in order before coming to the aid of the East.

It was fortunate that King William II of Sicily immediately sent a fleet to help those beleaguered Christian coastal fortresses. More fortunate had been the chance arrival of Conrad of Montferrat at Tyre within a fortnight of the Battle of Hattin. Unaware of the calamities that had befallen the Franks, Conrad was to be instrumental in the defence of that city before the forces of Saladin.

The first army of the Third Crusade to arrive in the East was that of the Holy Roman Emperor, Frederick Barbarossa. It was huge. The traditional chaos had broken out on the way to Constantinople, much to the chagrin of those princes unfortunate enough to have their lands crossed by this force. Things were no different in Constantinople where the Emperor Isaac Angelus's treaty with Saladin (primarily to keep the Seldjuks off his back while he dealt with the Norman foe in Greece) was as popular with the Germans as Frederick's suggestion for a Crusade against Constantinople was with the Byzantines.

What this massive German force under its old, wily emperor might have achieved will never be known since he was destined never to meet Saladin's forces. On the way to the Holy Land, Frederick would die while crossing a stream. The exact details are lost. One tale is that he fell from his horse, another that he drowned while trying to swim across. Whatever the true account might be, by the time Frederick was fished out of the water, he was dead. Without his leadership, the army fell apart under the traditional assaults of the East – Muslim skirmishers and disease. The bedraggled force that arrived was nothing to compare with what had set out months earlier. Frederick still accompanied it, although, fortunately, insensate to its sorry state. His companions had pickled him in vinegar, determined that he might complete his vow to reach the Holy City. Thus he entered Antioch in a barrel, although the heat and buffeting had managed to undo most of the preservative powers of the vinegar. The remaining mush was discreetly buried there but still a few of his late-followers, loyal to the last, stole some bones to accompany them on the journey south.

In the Holy Land these Germans were to meet up with new forces sent from Europe, under the command of two kings: Richard I of England, the Lion-

Heart, and Philip II of France. Of the two, Richard was the military man — he had recently attained the crown of England but had spent many of his years as a prince in combat, sometimes against his own father's forces. Although the younger of the two, Philip had ruled France for a decade and was very much the model of a medieval king.

Saladin had, by now, released King Guy. The Muslim leader had mistaken kingship for honour and had extracted a promise from Guy that he would no more take part in the conflict. Guy had reneged on this at the earliest opportunity. When he reached Tyre, however, a surprise was in store for him. Conrad considered the city he had saved to be his own and, no doubt minded of Guy's reputation, prevented him from entering. Guy and the forces he then managed to attract set off in consequence to attack Acre, keen to obtain a base from which he could plan the retrieval of his lost kingdom. Conrad was later to join him there and a peace was made between the two as they united to re-take Acre.

Conrad had brought with him Philip of France. They had landed at Acre to join the siege in April 1191. Apart from the extra men and ships, Philip had experts in siege technology with him, men whose knowledge of the trebuchet, the mangonel and other such catapults was to prove invaluable. God's Own Sling was already engaged in pounding the Muslim walls; the addition of the Evil Neighbour would further interrupt their already troubled sleep.

Richard, meanwhile, had been detained. A few of his ships had been forced by bad weather to seek safety at Cyprus. The island had recovered somewhat from Reynald's earlier attack. A Byzantine, Isaac Ducas Comnenus, had rebelled against his emperor (claiming that title for himself) and now ruled it independently. The hollowness of his claim was illustrated by the ease with which Richard dealt with him. One of the ships that landed had carried both Richard's sister and his fiancée – Berengaria of Navarre. Isaac obviously thought that he had rich fruit for the picking here. The two women had obvious hostage potential. Isaac, unaware of Richard's nature, made the worst decision. While failing to capture either of the women he displayed enough bad faith to antagonise Richard when he appeared with rest of the fleet. This was not difficult – if a competition had been held to elect the man with the shortest fuse in Europe at that time, then Richard would have been well placed. That King Guy and his leading barons had arrived pleading for Richard's help with the siege now taking place at Acre was of no importance. Richard flatly stated that Cyprus was of inestimable value to the Crusader cause. Isaac, for all his bravado, was swiftly beaten and captured. The natives rejoiced at the fall of a disliked leader. Richard left two of his men in charge and then set off for Acre with Guy, his men and the imprisoned former 'Emperor'. The native joy was soon to disperse as they were taxed to a new level and, more unforgivably in their eyes, legally shorn of the symbol of Eastern manhood – their beards.

Upon Richard's arrival the rulers of Acre despaired. The men and arms now set against them were considerable. The Franks and their allies were at first held up by disease (Philip and Richard both falling prey) and then by the inevitable bickering as Guy won over Richard to his cause and Conrad won Philip to his. This was not to hold them up for long. In July, Acre surrendered, offering up a fortune for the safety of its inhabitants. Saladin cursed his bad luck, unable to come to its rescue in time.

Once Acre was captured, the arguments between Guy and Conrad resumed. Guy, never popular, had found his hold on the throne loosened by the death of his wife, who provided his claim to the position. Conrad, cunningly, had married her sister in the meantime, and thus the Latin barons who favoured him (or rather could not stand Guy) had a legitimate argument in calling for his leadership. Finally, it was decided that Conrad would remain ruler of Beirut, Sidon and Tyre and that he (or his family, should he predecease) would inherit the kingship on Guy's death.

The internal conflict between these rulers, despite their perilous standing, could not have impressed their potential saviours from the West. Philip soon had had enough of the East. He decided, despite the arguments to the contrary, to depart for home, leaving Richard in charge. Richard had had enough too – of Acre. Unable to reach an accommodation with Saladin and keen to push on to Jerusalem, he had the thousands of Saracen prisoners from the siege killed. The Muslims were outraged. As the Crusaders slowly moved down the coast Saladin's forces regularly mounted attacks on them and eventually the real confrontation took place at Arsuf. At this battle the Muslim forces were defeated. Saladin withdrew with the intent of fighting another day, closer to Jerusalem. Richard's forces rejoiced at such a victory.

Months later, in 1192, Jerusalem had still not been taken. The joy at last year's victory had been replaced by sober thought. Richard was confident that he could take the Holy City. What was in doubt was whether it could be held. Saladin's forces had been proven not to be invincible. What was beyond question was that the native Christian forces could not hold onto much more than the coastal fortresses without a permanent and sizeable contribution from the West. Richard, however, had no intention of staying. He was there for the glory, for the riches to be won in battle – not for the administration and burden of maintaining a Latin Kingdom. Negotiations were protracted with the Muslim enemy; news began to arrive of troubles back home in England; Cyprus was proving to be a hot potato. Richard sold the latter to the Templars, hoping to rid himself of its troubles. Then the Templars wanted to sell it back. With these issues in mind, Richard took it upon himself to make Conrad king in the Holy Land and to arrange Guy's accession to the throne of Cyprus. Conrad's joy was short-lived. He was struck down by agents of the Assassins not far from the safety of his palace one April evening. Although the tool of his demise was known, the hand behind the blade was a subject of much speculation that year. Conspiracy theories abounded. Conrad's widow, Isabella, married a newcomer, Henry of Champagne, within days of his death. It was Henry who was to benefit from Richard's interference in the Latin succession.

Richard still delayed his leaving. Instead, his next move was to conquer the Muslim coastal fortress of Daron. The Christians now held a kingdom that stretched along the lengthy coast, a kingdom that was no wider than a ribbon. For all his own meagre talents as a king, Richard had proved one thing. As had been the case with the Muslims, a single, undisputed leader brought tremendous benefit to the Frankish cause. The rival barons might still plot against one another but the extremes of their behaviour were curtailed before him. The unfortunate realisation that came with this was that it was now difficult to see how Europe could hold the Holy Land beyond the short term. The lessons of recent history must have made it clear to Saladin that he did not need so much to engage in a war of aggression as to play a waiting game. Richard did himself no favours when he allowed news of his intention to leave to spread. Knowing this, Saladin could merely play for time. Even without this knowledge, it must have been apparent that any major force sent from Europe would, by its very nature, be a temporary upset to the reality that, under a single leader, the Muslims would inevitably reclaim the Frankish kingdoms. A war fought overseas for ideological reasons is one that is always going to be difficult to win, as the Americans were later to find in Vietnam. The Muslims weren't going anywhere – they had nowhere else to go. The Franks would never be in the ascendant, not without outside help from their fellow Christians whose hearts would remain in their European homelands.

Despite Richard's avowed intention to leave, and the endless negotiations, his finest hour as a military leader was yet to come. In 1192, hearing of an attack on Jaffa by Saladin's armies, Richard rushed with a smaller force to the scene. He not only recaptured the city but also, in the days afterwards, withstood an attack by Saladin's again numerically superior army who were trying to crush him before the appearance of reinforcements. Richard's behaviour here was indeed heroic, appearing wherever he was needed, thoughtless of personal risk. His older opponent could not but admire the man's courage, however much he despised his cruelty. This event at Jaffa was to be the final act of the Third Crusade however. In the negotiations that followed the demands put by Saladin could not be refused by a king so anxious about the state of his country in his absence. A peace was agreed, allowing both Christians and Muslims to move freely. Although Richard had been unable to take Jerusalem, he now ensured that Christians would be able to worship there, and pilgrims visit. That done, Richard departed for England. His journey home was to take some considerable time as he fell captive first to the Austrians and then the Germans. When he arrived back in 1194, his old adversary in the East, Saladin, had finally succumbed to sickness more than a year before.

After Saladin's death, the Muslim sense of unity dissipated. His lands were divided among his many sons and their internecine plotting gave the thin Latin Kingdoms breathing space. Saladin's brother, Al-Adil, struggled to keep his young nephews in line. Henry of Champagne, despite marrying Isabella, was never to be crowned king. In the years that followed Henry did his best to maintain the Frankish territory. The Assassins once more came on board. In the north the Armenians worried at Antioch with the tacit approval of the Christians in the south. Henry's one major antagonist within his own borders, Amalric of Lusignan, in control of Acre, would soon relinquish that territory when his elder brother, Guy of Cyprus, died in 1194, leaving the throne of the island vacant. Amalric withdrew there, biding his time. His opportunity was not long in coming. In 1197, Henry died in circumstances redolent of a black comedy. While receiving guests he stepped back through the open window of an upper level of his palace in Acre. The only help to hand was his loyal dwarf who, grasping hold of his beloved leader, took that loyalty to the grave as both plummeted to their deaths, storeys below. Amalric stepped forward to take the once-again widowed Isabella's hand, to general approbation.

That same year a force of Germans, eager to rescue their reputation from the debacle of their role in the Third Crusade arrived. They showed the traditional respect for the wisdom of the Christian rulers they found there and sought out the infidel as early as they could. By the close of the following year, most of them had returned to Europe. They had contributed to the taking of Beirut, a victory that owed more to the incompetence of those holding that city than any military genius on the part of the Franks. Apart from that single success, they had achieved nothing and the German contribution to the Frankish cause remained as ridiculed as it had been when they arrived. Some were sufficiently shamed to stay and, working with a hospice set up by German merchants in Acre, formed yet another Military Order – the Teutonic Knights. Another force was thus born, with the intention of providing help and the independence required to add further dissent in an already factionalised series of campaigns. As the new century dawned, news of another forthcoming European Crusade began to reach the East.

If the Third Crusade could be pointed to as the moment where myths of the valiant Crusader had at least some basis in fact, the Fourth could be described as the moment where they lost the plot. In 1202 the Fourth Crusade was officially launched as an attempt to recover Jerusalem. It soon descended into an opportunity to deal with those vile heretics in Constantinople. The next decade was remarkable for a series of Crusades against everybody but the Muslims: the cross was not only taken against the Byzantines but in the Baltic and, in France in 1209, against Cathar heretics. The one attempt against the Muslims was, bizarrely enough, made by children.

The Children's Crusade

Peter the Hermit, inspiration in the First Crusade, provided an example for other evangelists of the lower orders after his death. The Crusades were not necessarily an endeavour limited to the nobility. An inspirational speaker from any class could do his bit to contribute to the cause. Itinerant preachers who delivered this message were now a common fact of life, particularly among the towns and villages of Europe. Into this fervent arena came a twelve-year-old boy, Stephen, a French shepherd by trade, who claimed to have encountered Christ and to have been given a letter from him that authorised his role as a preacher of the Crusade, destined to win back the Holy Land. The French king, Philip, had little time – unsurprisingly – for such nonsense when the child arrived before him and sent him packing. Swiftly and inexplicably news of his mission spread and soon children across France were laying down their hoes and flocking to the banner of one who prophesied an army of children before whom the Mediterranean would part and the Saracen lay down his arms. Germany was not to be outdone in this regard – a child by the name of Nicholas began to preach a similar message there. Tens of thousands of children were soon migrating south. The French arrived at Marseilles; the Germans, in different waves, passed through Switzerland and eventually ended up at Genoa and Pisa. The Mediterranean unhelpfully refused to divide at either port. The German armies of children, and the dubious characters who followed in their wake, soon broke up in the face of the sea's obduracy. Many had died or were lost on the journey down, although a few of the wealthiest managed to obtain passage to the Holy Land at Genoa and Pisa. More went on to Rome, obtaining an audience with the Pope who indulged their fervency, promising that, when older, their commitment to the crusading cause would be allowed to blossom. Satisfied, they broke up to seek their immediate fortune elsewhere. Some embarked on the dangerous return home; others chose to stay in Italy, seeking more than the grim lives they had escaped from in Germany. The few parents who did get their children back were outnumbered by the angry many who, unable to seek redress in any other manner, chose to salve their wounds by hanging Nicholas's father for allowing his son to start such an escapade.

Unfortunately for the French children, a couple of enterprising merchants in Marseilles offered to provide their passage to Palestine. William the Pig and Hugh the Iron lived up to their word – they sold the children off to the Muslims as slaves. Twenty years were to pass before rumours of their fate in Egypt, in Baghdad and throughout the Maghrib were to make their way back to the few of their parents still living.

The Fourth Crusade

A new Pope, Innocent III, strongly supported the idea of a new Crusade. Preachers, fired up with the customary crusading zeal, went up and down France and Germany, preaching the cross. The concerns of kings were largely elsewhere but many barons flocked to the cause, hungry for land and booty elsewhere. The absence of any major figure, a Philip or even a Richard, to lead the effort was to become noticeable. One group wanted to attack Egypt, seeing it as the key to a successful reconquest; another, for personal reasons, wanted to attack Constantinople to replace the current ruler there. The Byzantine Empire's continued decline had made it impossible to follow the traditional overland route to the East. The only feasible way was by sea. The Italian republics were the only possible carriers and the Venetians offered the solution. Venice was enjoying marvellous success. With no concern but money, they were prepared to do any deal – with the devil himself if need be. In Constantinople they bought trading rights cheaply, playing on the desperate need for money there. In the Levant, they carried essentials to the Franks and relieved them of their Eastern luxuries. In Egypt they negotiated with the Muslims, keen to raise funds themselves. Venice had a thumb for every pie. When the crusading transport deal was done, however, the Venetians suddenly found themselves struggling to find a place to deliver these fighters where their own interests would not be likely to suffer. After much procrastination, they tried to convince the Crusaders to start their campaign by reclaiming Venetian territory that had fallen to the Hungarians (fellow Christians) along the Dalmatian coast and, in particular, the city of Zara. Faced with bankruptcy at the cost of maintaining their stay in Venice, or the option of swimming to Jerusalem, the Crusaders had no choice but to acquiesce. They sacked Zara in 1202. When news came back to Innocent that his holy army's first act had been against their co-religionists he blew his top. Excommunication, a tool that was to feature entertainingly in later Crusades, became the way in which his displeasure was shown. Both the Venetians and the Crusaders were punished in this way. The Crusaders' excommunication, however, was soon rescinded when Innocent calmed down and realised both that they had been given no other option by their hosts and that the force could hardly continue without Papal support. Innocent's control of the campaign, however, had been shown to be illusory.

Behind the push towards Constantinople was Philip of Swabia, whose wife was the daughter-in-law of the displaced Emperor of the Byzantines. Restoring her family to the throne there might maintain his marital bliss and, if it gave him a chance to make a little bit of money at the same time, what was wrong with that? Philip had already been excommunicated prior to the Zara escapade. What more could the Pope do? The crusading army, for all it had done in Zara, still owed its host and transporters. The Venetians began to see the appeal of a redirection towards Constantinople. Why bother paying for the right to trade when they could get this bunch of fools to fight to claim those rights for them, and more, pay the Venetians for the opportunity to do it? For now, the Venetians pressed their claims strongly, and news that the pretender to the Byzantine throne would pay these debts swayed many otherwise upright Crusaders. The few that had rectitude enough – or at least the money to afford such a thing – paid their own way to Syria. The rest set off, under Venetian sails, towards Constantinople. In his palace, Innocent raged, powerless to alter the course of his instrument of salvation.

After a few attempts by the Crusaders, the incumbent Emperor, Alexius III, upped and fled. Philip's cousin by marriage was raised to the throne as Alexius IV, sharing it with his father, the tortured and blinded ex-Emperor Isaac who had been dug up out of the bowels of the Byzantine gaols by those left in charge of the city after Alexius III had departed. Alexius IV's joy was brought to an end when he tried to pay the Crusaders and, through them, the Venetians. The money wasn't there. He tried to bring in harsh taxes to placate the cocky westerners who now walked through the city as if it were their own. His people rioted. A new Emperor, Alexius V, was installed and the old pair imprisoned and tortured to death. If this had meant their money would have been forthcoming then the Crusaders would probably not have minded. As it was, they decided enough was enough. Clearly the only Emperor of Constantinople who could be trusted to pay up would be a western Emperor.

It took the Crusaders relatively little effort in the end to break the city. Once in, they unleashed their pent-up aggression in a way that was to make the Byzantines wish that the Muslims had been their conquerors instead. Alexius V had fled by the time these barbarians poured in. For three days they ravaged the city. The women they raped, the men and children they killed; everything they could steal they did and what they couldn't take, they destroyed. Much is made of what was lost in the final sack of Constantinople by the Ottoman Sultan Mehmed II in 1453, but the damage done in 1204 was greater. The ancient statue of Athena by Phidias, a sculpture that had lasted centuries and dated back to the Athens of Socrates and Plato, had been broken up by supporters of Alexius V in his efforts to supplant the previous ruler. Its destruction had been an omen of the devastation to come. The Venetians and the Barons leading the Crusade finally reined their troops in when they realised that they would have nothing left if the rampage continued. They elected a ruler, Baldwin of Flanders, pragmatically supported by the Venetians as a candidate too weak to oppose their activities in the lands that he was to rule. For the next few years many more of the great treasures of Constantinople were to flood onto the European market.

The Venetians claimed parts of Constantinople, the western coast of Greece and many of its islands. Baldwin, in addition, sold them Crete. The Venetians were content to franchise out nearly all of the Aegean Isles. Mainland Greece was entirely given over to westerners. There was now a Duke of Athens from Burgundy; a Prince of Achaea from France. In the north-west, in Epirus, one Byzantine lord held out. In the east a host of small Byzantine states claimed independence – in Niceaea and in Trebizond on the Black Sea, among others. With these bastions of Byzantine power intact, the population of Constantinople could always hold out hope that one day a Byzantine would again occupy the throne.

When news of this reached Innocent it put him in a quandary. His anger at the direction the Crusade had taken was subdued by his joy at the final reduction of the Byzantine heresy. Rome stood unchallenged. When news of the sack of the city and the barbarous behaviour displayed by the Crusaders arrived it shocked him. News of how cunningly the Venetians had exploited the situation brought back his anger. Still, he had the hope that now the real job could continue. When he found out that his own legate on the Crusade had announced that the successful capture of the Byzantine Empire meant that those who had made the promise to go to the Latin Kingdoms to rescue Jerusalem could now go home, the news nearly finished him off. The Fourth Crusade was officially over.

In the East, the non-appearance of the rumoured Great Crusade was now explained by the news that began to come through to both the Muslims and Christians there. Peace reigned for the present. Amalric had come to an agreement with Al-Adil. Each had his preoccupations. Amalric was to die in 1205 with the peace still in force. News of the taking of Constantinople not only meant the end to any immediate help for the Franks. It provided a magnet for those minor nobility in the Latin Kingdoms who had still failed to make their name and fortune. Land and opportunity beckoned much closer to Europe, in the western parts of the old Byzantine Empire, now renamed Romania by its conquerors. How much easier a prospect that must have seemed than continuing to hope against hope for something to turn up in the Muslim badlands. Knights began to make their way to the 'new' Empire. The wisest among the Franks received the news of the independent Byzantine states with dismay. After the sack of their capital, how could these rulers wish for anything else but the destruction of western hopes in the Latin Kingdoms? How, also, could any future Crusade ever make its way across Asia Minor now? It was not quite the end – but where could they go from here?

Part 4

Later Crusades

Later Crusades

The Fifth Crusade

The saviour of the Fifth Crusade was always hoped to be Frederick II, the German Holy Roman Emperor. Despite his promises, he never made it over for this engagement. His was to be the deciding role instead in the Sixth. Inspired still by Richard of England's earlier observation that Egypt was the key to the retrieval of the Latin territories, the Fifth Crusade started in North Egypt – and ended there. At the heart of the Fifth Crusade is again a tale of divided leadership. The Muslims were too split to repel the invaders easily. After their initial gains, the Christians were too disunited to get any further. A strong Papal representative, Pelagius, presumed himself to be in charge and provided a constant impediment to the overall military leader, John of Brienne. John was a latecomer to the East. Upon Amalric's death, the crown had passed back to his widow, Isabella, briefly; with her death her eldest daughter, Maria, in her teens, ascended the throne with John, Lord of Beirut, appointed regent. John of Brienne was already an old man when he was pushed forward by Philip of France as a suitable husband for the teenage Queen. He quickly adapted to the political realities of the East; his age, perhaps, encouraged a certain circumspection on his part. His modest achievements were shown under a favourable light when compared to the situation to the north.

Antioch was in a mess. The legitimacy of its ruler, Bohemond IV, was challenged by the claims of his nephew, Raymond. Raymond on his own would have provided a minor obstacle. Unfortunately the case was backed by his relative, the powerful Armenian lord, Leo. Every force involved in the area soon found itself on one side or the other. The Templars, the Seldjuk Turks and the Antiochene Greeks supported Bohemond; the Hospitallers and Al-Adil were behind Leo. Bohemond struggled to put down revolt in his other territory, Tripoli. Leo cunningly put the Armenian Church under the Pope. Bohemond sided with the Greek Church. With the Pope's blessing Bohemond and Antioch were excommunicated for a while and then the Churches switched their allegiances. The Templars' role as Christian supremacists was now challenged by extremist behaviour from the Hospitallers as they began to use the Assassins as tools. They first took out Bohemond's eldest son in church and then followed this up by killing the Patriarch of Jerusalem. A kind of calm only settled when Raymond took control in a coup in Antioch while Bohemond was sorting out Tripoli. The whole episode was a per-

fect example of interests cutting across religious ties
in the East.

That John of Brienne, a lowly member of the
French nobility, was to take command of the Crusade
is a comment on the tenacity of kings. Frederick II
never made it over for the Fifth Crusade. The young
King of Cyprus, Hugh, died on the way there. King
Andrew of Hungary treated the whole thing as a holi-
day – the petrified head of Saint Stephen being the
main souvenir he brought home before the attack on
Egypt was even launched. As it was, the forces that
landed in Egypt in 1218 comprised a combination of
French, Austrians, members of the Military Orders
(Templars, Hospitallers and Teutonic Knights), natives
of Outremer and a smattering of others. Their plan
was to take the fortress of Damietta close to the coast
where its eponymous branch of the Nile flowed into
the sea. It was on a piece of land almost entirely sur-
rounded by water, with the river to the west and the
great Lake Manzaleh to the east. Damietta was not to
fall until November 1219, when the Crusaders finally
broke in to find a community wasted by disease and
death. Beyond this, little was achieved. A final push
south was made in 1221 where the Christians took
Sharimshah.

John argued that they stop and consolidate; Pelagius
demanded that they push on. They did and found
themselves surrounded. The Nile had risen as it sea-
sonally did; the Muslims opened the gates holding the

water back. The Crusaders fell back in confusion, flooded and harried by the Muslim forces. Pelagius was forced to sue for peace and the Fifth Crusade ended when the Christians left in their ships in September that year. Opportunities had frequently come the Crusaders' way. More than once the Muslims had offered to cede Jerusalem and its surroundings to the Christians during the campaign. Pelagius had always refused. John's attempts to take command were in part hindered by his worries back home in Outremer. In addition, the legitimacy of his leadership was regularly undermined by Pelagius, with his constant taunts that soon a real ruler, Frederick II, would come to take command. A greater man than John might have firmly sidelined Pelagius and, having done so, would have had a real chance to take control of Egypt. This thought must have occurred to the Crusaders who survived as they set sail for Europe. One great man had been present among the Christians – Saint Francis of Assisi had arrived in an attempt to bring peace in 1219. The Muslim leader, the Sultan al-Kamil, listened to his entreaties, offered him gifts, and then sent him on his way. It was probably a more gracious reception than the one he received from his own side.

The Sixth Crusade

The days of the early Crusades appeared to be simpler times. There had always been internal conflicts on both sides but, in general, a more straightforward set of circumstances existed. With each subsequent endeavour the waters of the East muddied. The alliance between Assassin and Hospitaller would have been unthinkable generations earlier. It is, perhaps, noteworthy that the final recapture of Jerusalem would fall to a man whom, more than any other, encapsulated the complexities of the time. The brief resurgence in Christian fortunes would be down to a figure best described in modern terms as an anti-hero.

Frederick II was an extraordinary figure: he truly contained multitudes. He was raised in Sicily and elected king there at the age of three. Sicily's multi-cultural heritage informed his development. His brilliant mind soaked up whatever he was exposed to – he gained fluency in Arabic, French, German, Greek, Italian and Latin. His exposure to the Islamic heritage of that island and his genius provided him with the mindset to deal with the Muslims of the East in a manner more common among the native Christian leaders of Outremer. In this he was unique as a Western leader. Typical of the contradictions within him were that, as the greatest secular defender of the faith, he employed a bodyguard of Saracens – who were thus immune to Papal seduction – before he ever set foot in Outremer. His greatest flaws were mixed in with his strengths in the way in which he transcended the typical European king. Frederick saw himself as above everyone, including the Pope. If he had been born

Emperor of the Byzantines it would have been a different matter. If the Papacy had been weaker and if the lesser kings and nobility had not grown used to the powers and privileges they enjoyed in the thirteenth century, then his achievements might have been more lasting. That his success in the East was limited is perhaps understandable when one considers how he saw the Papacy as the real villain rather than Islam. And the Papacy's later description of him as Anti-Christ is testimony enough of how much of a threat they saw him to be.

The first half of Frederick's life is the story of his struggle to regain his father's position as Holy Roman Emperor. Part of his coronation as Emperor involved a promise to take up the cross. While his old tutor, Honorius III, was Pope, Frederick's protestations of needing to put his own lands in order before sorting out others fell on friendly ears. When Honorious died, and the new Pope Gregory IX was elected, it became clear that this argument was not going to work. Gregory insisted he go. When malaria affected both Frederick and the army he had gathered, Gregory promptly excommunicated him for his dilatoriness. It is ironic that at this point the Sultan al-Kamil, one of the architects of the repelling of the Fifth Crusade, was in secret communication with Frederick. He, too, urged the Emperor to come to the Holy Land, hoping that Frederick would join forces with him against a threat to his own security from the east.

Frederick was not a man to let a little thing like excommunication stand in his way, despite the fact that, technically, it made him ineligible to take part in a Crusade. Since his election as Emperor, he now also had a personal interest in Outremer. In 1222, John of Brienne had journeyed to Europe to seek support for Outremer and, in particular, to ensure the succession by finding a husband for his daughter, Yolanda, now Queen after the death of her mother. Frederick seemed the perfect choice – a decision encouraged by Pope Honorius as one likely to hurry the Emperor's journey to the East. Once the marriage had taken place, Frederick bundled off his young bride to Sicily where she remained for the rest of her short life. John found himself extra to requirements and, when the opportunity arose to act as regent at Constantinople, he hurriedly accepted. Frederick could thus claim the throne of Jerusalem by right before leaving Europe.

When Frederick arrived in 1228, his claim had effectively vanished. Yolanda's death after giving birth to their son, Conrad, was now common knowledge. By rights the throne was in the possession of the infant – Frederick was merely regent until Conrad came of age. To Frederick this was of little importance since he was the *de facto* ruler. To the Barons of Outremer, this was of the greatest importance. Before even reaching Acre, Frederick was throwing his weight around. His arrival at Cyprus, and his demands to see there the leading nobles of both the island and the mainland had considerably unsettled them. He was, after all, Holy Roman Emperor and thus overlord of the isle. His bullying manner with the barons was to be counter-productive. Later they would look for any excuse not to co-operate with him, while being wary of deliberate and obvious disobedience. The perfect excuse came soon after he arrived in Acre. News began to drift in that, not content with the first excommunication for failing to leave promptly enough, Gregory had excommunicated him a second time for daring to go on a crusade while excommunicated. Regardless of Gregory's logic, or of queries over how, exactly, an excommunicate could be excommunicated, the barons could legally shun him. Certainly the Templars and Hospitallers were keen not to earn the Pope's enmity here – though the Teutonic Knights, with their German origins, were caught between a rock and a very hard place indeed.

Frederick had his friends to fall back on – not surprisingly, they were all German. And too few to provide enough of an army to retake Jerusalem by force. Frederick must have wondered what he had entangled himself in. To be ruler of the Holy Land, to be the one who took back Jerusalem was fodder for his ego and a powerful boost to his prestige in his battle against the one figure he felt was a threat to his role as the Lord of Christian Europe – the Pope. Now he was actually in Outremer, the material benefits must have seemed slight. He had effectively outmanoeuvred himself by his own actions. He could not move forward, nor could he retreat without a massive loss of face. The only recourse open to him was negotiation with the enemy.

He was in luck. The Sultan al-Kamil shared his pragmatism. Al-Kamil was preoccupied with the familiar concern of unification – in his case, of the separate Ayubite territories. In addition, he was still concerned about the threat from the east, from Jelal ad-Din and his Khwarismian Turks who had recently defeated the new threat coming out of the Far East, the Mongols. Al-Kamil and Frederick held each other in mutual respect. Handing over Jerusalem and a few of the other sites, Bethlehem and Nazareth among them, was nothing if it allowed al-Kamil to forget about any Frankish threat. However, ensuring the Muslim possession of the Islamic sites within Jerusalem, such as the Dome of the Rock and the area around the Temple, was essential to his reputation. What did this matter to Frederick? Al-Kamil also played safe by offering only the tiniest strip of land to link these places with the Latin coast. It would be an impossible territory to defend, should he ever desire to retake these places. Frederick couldn't really care less. It gave him the solution to his immediate problems, particularly if it took care of his critics. On 18 February 1229, the agreement was signed, and for the last time, Jerusalem passed back into the ownership of the west. Al-Kamil and Frederick celebrated the fruition of their plan.

Unity between Muslim and Christian at this level had never occurred in the East until this point. Now a common response issued from both sides. Pious believers across the divide went crazy. Al-Kamil faced harsh criticism from his own people over the cowardly seceding of Islamic territory to unbelievers. Frederick faced even more abuse. That he had won such an indefensible territory, saddling them with a strategic nightmare, enraged the native barons; that he had left the Muslims in control of parts of Jerusalem seemed an act of treachery to the truest of believers; that he had out-foxed the Church and, despite two excommunications, had actually won back the jewel of the Christian East sent the Roman Church into apoplexy. The Patriarch of Jerusalem itself, Gerold of Lausanne, was moved to immediate action. A third excommunication was unlikely to cut much mustard with Frederick. Gerold instead declared that, if Jerusalem were to receive its regent and liberator, he would place an interdict upon the whole city, banning any church ceremony or acts taking place there until further notice.

Frederick went to the city, and, in spite of his son's claim, declared himself King of Jerusalem. He had to crown himself as no priest would do the deed. After the ceremony, Frederick went walkabout. On noticing a priest following him into a Muslim holy place he ordered the man removed and declared that any others who entered without Muslim approval should be executed. In the Dome of the Rock, a grille was explained as necessary to keep the sparrows out. Using a Muslim description for Christians he remarked that, 'God has now sent you pigs'. News of these comments, and of his self-enthronement, added to the odium in which the Franks held him.

Frederick retired, exasperated by the ungrateful response. News of problems in his European lands began to reach him. The Pope was taking advantage of his absence to make a move on his Italian possessions. Frederick, after making public his plans to leave, tried to slip away unnoticed under the cover of darkness. News of his leaving spread and such was the hatred of him held by even commoners that he was forced to flee for his ship under an unholy rain of excrement and rotting offal hurled by the crowd.

So ended the Sixth Crusade.

The Seventh Crusade

After Frederick left, although the Barons attempted to rebuild the defences around Jerusalem and the other sites he had regained, many of their fears were realised. It was impossible to defend much of the territory from the depredations of bandits and bands of Muslims angry at al-Kamil's perfidy. Back in Europe, Frederick had managed to come to a temporary understanding with the Pope in 1230. Divisions existed between the commanders he had left and the native barons, led by the powerful and respected John of Ibelin, ruler of Beirut, in league with the young King Henry of Cyprus. Attempts were made to dispute Frederick's kingship in Jerusalem, particularly by Queen Alice of Cyprus. With the death of John in a riding accident, and the absence of the true king, Frederick's infant son, Conrad, practical government was in the hands of the Commune of Acre – a group of leading barons and merchants in the chief Latin city. This control was disputed by Frederick's appointed representatives or *bailli*, who endeavoured to rule in his name. Particularly hated was Richard Filangieri, sent by Frederick from Italy in 1231 – so much so that he achieved the rare feat of bringing the Templars and Hospitallers together in common cause against him. To the north, too, in Antioch, a commune made most of the decisions, regardless of the desires expressed by their weak lord, Bohemond V.

The Ayubites were briefly united under al-Kamil. Chaos broke out after his death in 1238. The threats posed by Jelal ad-Din were removed by a greater one as the unknown terror-to-come, the Mongols, further penetrated his eastern borders. The end of Frederick and al-Kamil's peace came and a small crusading force, led by Tibald of Champagne and the Duke of Burgundy, prompted by the Pope, arrived in Acre in 1239. Apart from their involvement in the recovery of Ascalon on the coast, and a bit of banditry, little was achieved. Tibald returned to Europe the following year with most of his men. The Templars and Hospitallers fell out again; this time to the extent that physical violence occurred between the members of the two orders when they met in public. Both were resented by the commoners as each operated without control, pursuing schemes which often ended with as many Christian deaths as Muslim. The continued absence of Conrad pushed the barons to finally appoint Alice and her husband, Ralph, as regents until the day should come when Conrad would sail out to claim his kingdom. The hope was that this would bring some degree of stability. The reality was that the pair had no control over the barons that had selected them. The Military Orders continued to scheme, with the Templars replacing their holier-than-thou policy with a new one of intervention in Muslim politics. At first their efforts were handsomely rewarded when they won back the Temple from the Muslims by cunning negotiations. Cocky with success, they then tried to intercede in a war between two Muslim princes.

Ayub, the leader out of Egypt, the one the Templars schemed against, had his own plan to repay the interference. Since Jelal ad-Din's death his Khwarismian Turks had meandered throughout the region, indulging in a little sporadic pillaging. Ayub wrote and offered them Jerusalem and the surrounding areas. Ten thousand armed horsemen answered his invitation. Thus was Jerusalem finally lost, in 1244. The refugees poured out and tried to make their way west.

Few escaped the depredations of the bandits who roamed the paths to the Frankish coast.

Meanwhile the cream of the Frankish forces sallied out to meet their Muslim allies. Together they met Ayub's army, strengthened by the Khwarismian Turks outside the village of La Forbie. The Franks had backed the wrong side and were devastated in the ensuing battle. In a later incident the Khwarismian Turks turned against Ayub and were similarly destroyed. It was cold comfort for the Franks. Ayub's position was unchallenged in the Islamic world and he could turn his attention to the Franks who had dared to scheme against him. He was content for now to level Ascalon after a siege.

In 1248, under the command of Louis IX of France, a man revered for his piety, the forces of the Seventh Crusade arrived at Cyprus. This Crusade was very much a one-man affair. As supportive of the endeavour as the Papacy was, its main concern at that time was keeping Frederick in check. After much deliberation, the decision was made to strike at the heart of Ayub's kingdom: Egypt. They arrived in 1249 and, with admirable alacrity, captured Damietta. The rising floodwaters of the Nile delayed them for a few months and, when the Crusaders tried to push south, they found a Muslim army ready to oppose them. The two armies hesitated to confront each other for some time. When they finally clashed, outside the town of al-Mansura, the Crusaders' victory was bought with

the lives of many of their men. The Muslims had punished them with their elite mercenary force, the
Mameluks, who drove the Christians back when they
tried to break into the town itself. By then Ayub had
died of natural causes, after an offer of Jerusalem for
the return of Damietta – an offer that Louis rejected,
much as Pelagius had before him. Ayub's son,
Turanshah, had yet to arrive to take command when
the Muslims struck again at the Crusaders. Louis'
forces held out. It was clear, however, that the losses
they had sustained in both battles would prevent them
pressing further with the Crusade. An attempt to
retreat went horribly wrong. The Muslims struck once
more, this time capturing more prisoners than they
knew what to do with, including the saintly but hapless Louis. The ransom was huge and, when it was
paid, Louis departed for Outremer, awaiting the
release of the rest of his companions, while many of
those freed with him went back to France. Turanshah
was not celebrating. He was dead, killed in a coup carried out by his Mameluk officers.

Louis stayed in Outremer until 1254, doing what he
could before departing for France. Afterwards, an
internal struggle occurred that outdid the brawling
between Military Orders. In 1256, competition
between Genoa and Venice irrupted into armed confrontation. This war carried on for years and dragged
in most of the barons of the region. Beyond
Outremer, in Constantinople, the Venetians con-

trolled trade. As a consequence, the Genoese supplied aid to the Nicaean Byzantine Emperor, Michael Paleologus, in his attempts to recapture that city, and hence the old Empire. He succeeded in 1261 and the Genoese reaped the commercial rewards of a trading monopoly.

Outremer struggled on in increasing disarray. No more Crusades would be sent out from Europe. The Mongols were beginning to make their presence felt. They had, in fact, already wiped out the Assassins in their Persian headquarters in 1257. In 1258, they sacked Baghdad. Eighty thousand people died there. Christians rejoiced at the news yet they were uncertain as to what would happen when the Mongols finally reached the Levantine coast. The devastation that they had caused in Europe some twenty years earlier – getting as far as the Adriatic – was at the back of Frankish minds. The Mongols pushed on west. Many Muslim lords were disposed to pay them homage once news got around of what happened to those who refused. The Prince of Mayyafaraqin was one of those who did refuse. The Mongols, once they captured his city, killed him by forcing him to eat his own flesh. When they reached Antioch, the Christians paid the Mongol leader, Hulagu, due deference and were repaid by the restoration of territories previously won from the Franks by the Muslims. The Christians were jubilant. In 1260, Damascus had no other choice but to go over to the Mongols. News that Christians had accompanied the Mongol army from Antioch and Armenia when it rode into the city percolated through the Arab world. It was one more thing to hold against the Christians.

The final confrontation came that year, at Ain Jalud. News that the Mongol leadership and part of their army had been drawn back east to sort out a question of succession gave the Muslims one last chance. They took it. A Mameluk army came out of Egypt to confront the Mongols. Everything was at stake. If they lost, then the Mongols could have ridden all the way to Morocco before encountering opposition. The whole future of Islam lay in the balance.

The Battle of Ain Jalud was hard-fought but, at the end, the Muslims, under their Sultan Qutuz, prevailed. The tide had turned. In what was becoming a tradition, Qutuz had little time to enjoy his role as Saviour of Islam. One of his lieutenants, Baibars, who had won respect at Ain Jalud, assassinated his master and assumed his role. The Franks would come to curse his name.

Part 5

The Fall of Acre and Afterwards

The Fall of Acre and Afterwards

The Destruction of Outremer and the Fall of Acre

Initially Baibars had to strengthen his own position in
relation to the other Muslim leaders. Hulagu was still
occupied in the east but it became clear that as many,
if not more, Mongol leaders were converting to Islam
than Christianity. Factional squabbling among the
Mongols strengthened Baibars' cause. He began to
pick at Frankish territory. The town of Caesarea and
the Castle of Arsuf fell in 1265. The Castle of Safed
followed in 1266, the same year he defeated the
Armenians, paying them back for their support of the
Mongols by destroying their capital and taking forty
thousand prisoner. Baibars played a game of terror.
Truces made were broken when he attacked those
leaving a castle under the mistaken idea that they had
safe passage. Captives were slaughtered, their skulls
left heaped as proof of the fate awaiting those who displeased him. Through all this the coastal cities of
Outremer still rang to the sound of Venetians setting
on Genoese, and vice versa.

In 1268 Baibars finally got his revenge on those who

had been alongside the Armenians and Mongols – the Christians of Antioch. The Mameluks slew or took as slaves all but the richest, whom they ransomed. The treasure taken was such that 'coins were so plentiful that they were handed out in bowlfuls'. Antioch was never the same again after this devastation. With its loss, the Military Orders gave up the immediate surrounding castles and fortresses as they fled to safer ground. The remaining Assassins turned to Baibars' cause and he employed them with skill against the Christians. A small force from Spain arrived to help the Franks and then returned, having achieved nothing. Baibars continued to pick off Frankish and Templar and Hospitaller castles until Outremer was nothing more than scattered coastal fortresses. He now turned his attention back towards the Mongols. The Franks were merely annoying in the manner that insects were and he agreed a truce of ten years' peace with them in 1271, his attention firmly on the East.

Whether anything could have been made of this breathing space is purely speculative. In Europe the desperate situation in the East was noted and much commented upon yet no one would do anything practical about it. In Outremer the feuding continued: between Venetian and Genoese and between Templar and Hospitaller. The reigning monarch, Hugh III, King of Jerusalem and Cyprus, got so fed up with the infighting that in 1276 he upped and abandoned the mainland for Cyprus. Initially he could not even be bothered to leave someone else in charge. The only good news was the death of Baibars in 1277.

Qalawun succeeded him. By 1285 he had started to carry on where Baibars had left off. He had negotiated a truce with part of Outremer in 1283 and, two years later, he was striking at the parts not covered by it. The Hospitaller castle at Marqab was taken first. Now the Pisans started on the Genoese. The prospects for Outremer were so obviously bleak that even certain Mongols opposed to the Muslims sent an ambassador to Europe to plead for a Crusade – with no result. Meanwhile, in 1287, Qalawun took Lattakieh. The Venetians and their allies went as far as to urge Qalawun to attack Tripoli to get their revenge on the Genoese there. Qalawun readily complied. The destruction of Tripoli was complete. In 1289 Qalawun killed all the men and enslaved the women and children. A few escaped to Cyprus but others who tried to flee in small boats were slain in the surf where the Mameluk horsemen caught them. Qalawun levelled the city while the bodies rotted around it.

This dire news brought forth the slimmest of responses from Europe. A rabble of drunks, peasants and paupers was shipped out of Italy, courtesy of the Venetians. When they arrived at Acre they set upon the first Muslims they found, merchants and farmers who they identified as Muslims on the basis that they were the ones with beards. The thin truce that still held between Acre and Qalawun was torn up at this, such was the latter's anger. His death was the briefest of postponements. His dying words were commands to his son to carry on with his intention to take Acre. Al-Ashraf kept the promise he made to his father.

Over a hundred thousand men appeared outside Acre in 1291. Al-Ashraf brought other weapons with him: a pair of huge catapults called Victorious and Furious. Engineers worked to bring down the walls and a constant rain of arrows and crude bombs fell on the defenders within. Eventually, despite heroic resistance, the Mameluks broke through. The defenders, Templars and Hospitallers and Franks, fought side by side as more and more of the enemy poured into the city. They were driven back towards the quays but their resistance gave time for others to take to the sea and flee. By the time the Mameluks had finished, there were few left living to pass into the slave markets of the East. Again, as was the case with Tripoli, Qalawun destroyed as much of the city as he could, determined that it could never be used again should the Christians ever attempt to return. This was in May and, by the middle of August, Tyre, Sidon, Beirut and Haifa had all fallen. The last castles of the Military Orders had been evacuated. With the exception of the Templar castle on the tiny island of Ruad, just off the coast, the Franks had been wiped from the map of the East. Those few lucky enough to escape, and unlucky enough not to be able to find sanctuary in Europe, crowded Cyprus as refugees.

None of them would ever return.

Afterwards

So what had it all achieved? The answer is – very little. The financial costs were enormous to both sides, let alone the cost in human lives. Only the Italian city-states benefited from the trading opportunities that occurred. The cost to the rest of Europe has been accused of delaying the emergence of the Renaissance.

The barbarities committed by the Franks inspired the same behaviour from the Muslims and the memory of the Frankish acts profoundly changed the relationship between Islam and Christianity, down to the present day. In the end the forces of Islam were to emerge even more triumphant – from a tiny area in Asia Minor, the Ottoman Turks were to emerge. They would rise to form an empire that would eventually, in 1453, bring about the final end of the Byzantine Empire when they captured Constantinople. The Empire they founded would last until the twentieth century and they would occupy the Balkans for centuries, in a reversal of the Christians' occupation of the Holy Land. The Holy Land itself would finally pass from the control of the Ottomans after the end of the First World War to the British in 1920 under the Peace Treaty of Sèvres. The creation of Israel followed in 1948.

The Crusades continued in Europe, both in Livonia in the Baltic where the Teutonic Knights pursued the heathens for years to come and as a tool to strike against heretics within Europe. European struggles against the Turks in the centuries to come were still often seen and described as Crusades.

The Templars came to a sticky end not long after the fall of Acre. They were accused of blasphemy, their vast wealth divided among the Hospitallers and the rulers who acquiesced in their prosecution. Their last Grand Master, Jacques de Molay, was burnt at the stake in 1314.

The Hospitallers preserved themselves by staying out of reach of avaricious kings, first in Rhodes, and then in Malta. It was to be Napoleon who dislodged them from that island in 1798. Thereafter, they became a ceremonial order, which lasts to this day.

The Crusades became the stuff of legend in Europe. The exploits of the Crusader knights were celebrated in the Romantic period in painting and literature. The image persisted of the chivalrous knight, wearing a red cross, heroically doing battle with the Infidel.

Frederick II was to lose his battle with the Papacy; within thirty years of his death his heirs had lost the same battle. The German people never forgot him and many believed he was not dead but slept, much as the folktales of Arthurian legend declared that Arthur rested, waiting to come to the aid of his country in its time of trial.

Chronology

Date	Event
638	Capture of Jerusalem by the Caliph Omar.
1095	Pope Urban II preaches the First Crusade at Clermont (November).
1096	Launch of the First Crusade. Two armies comprising the 'People's Crusade' led by Peter the Hermit and Walter the Penniless, arrive in advance of the official armies led by a group of nobles, Raymond of Toulouse and Bohemond of Taranto senior among them.
1098	Edessa captured (March). Antioch captured (June).
1099	Jerusalem captured (July).
1144	Fall of Edessa to Zangi (December). News of its fall on reaching Europe provides the impetus for the Second Crusade.
1147	Launch of the Second Crusade by Pope Eugenius III, under the overall command of Louis VII of France and Conrad of Germany. Islamic forces led by Zangi's son, Nur ed-Din.
1149	End of the Second Crusade.

1187 Battle of Hattin (July).

Jerusalem falls to Saladin (October).

Pope Gregory VIII calls for the Third Crusade in response. Three rulers – Richard I of England, Philip II of France and the Holy Roman Emperor Frederick I – are to take part, with their respective forces.

1190 Frederick I dies leading his army in Cilicia.

1191 Cyprus falls to Richard I.

Acre falls to Richard I and Philip II.

1192 Third Crusade ends with the Treaty of Jaffa.

1202 The Fourth Crusade finally gets under way, four years after its proclamation by Pope Innocent III.

Zara taken by the Crusaders from the Hungarians (November).

1204 Constantinople sacked by Crusaders.

End of the Fourth Crusade.

1212 The Children's Crusade.

1218 The Fifth Crusade. A motley army under John of Brienne lands in Egypt.

Siege of Damietta.

1221 The Fifth Crusade ends, defeated by al-Kamil.

1228 The Sixth Crusade. The Holy Roman Emperor Frederick II arrives in the Levant.

1229 Jerusalem won back through Frederick II's diplomacy (February). The Crusade ends with his departure for Europe, later that year.

1249 The Seventh Crusade, under Louis IX of

France, lands in Egypt. Damietta captured.

1250   Seventh Crusade ends with defeat at al-Mansura. Louis stays on for four more years in Palestine before heading home.

1258   Mongols sack Baghdad.

1260   Battle of Ain Jalud – the Mongols defeated by the Mameluks.

1268   Antioch captured by Mameluks.

1291   The last remaining Frankish territory (including Acre and Beirut) in the East falls to the Islamic forces under Qalawun.

Further Reading

Eric Christiansen, *The Northern Crusades*, 2nd edn., (London: 1998)

Edward Gibbon, *The History of the Decline and Fall of the Roman Empire*, 3 vols., (Penguin)

Jonathan Harris, *Byzantium and the Crusades*, (London: 2003)

Norman Housley, *The Later Crusades, 1274–1580*, (Oxford: 1992)

Joinville and Villehardouin, *Chronicles of the Crusades*, (Penguin)

Amin Maalouf, ed., *The Crusades through Arab Eyes*, (London: 1984)

Zoë Oldenbourg, *The Crusades*, (London: 2001)

Jonathan Phillips, *The Fourth Crusade and the Sack of Constantinople*, (London: 2004)

Jean Richard, *The Crusades*, (Cambridge University Press)

Jonathan Riley-Smith, ed., *The Oxford History of the Crusades*, (Oxford: 1999)

S. Runciman, *A History of the Crusades*, 3 vols., (Cambridge: 1951–4)

K.M. Setton (editor), *A History of the Crusades*, 2nd edn., 6 vols. (Madison, Wis.: 1969–89)

Jonathan Sumption, *The Albigensian Crusade*, (London: 1999)

William Watson, *The Last of the Templars*, (London: 1992)

Index